The Second Grand Lodge

The Grand Lodge of Ireland,
the London Irish &
Antients Freemasonry

The Second Grand Lodge

The Grand Lodge of Ireland, the London Irish & Antients Freemasonry

Ric Berman

The Old Stables Press
• Oxfordshire •
2023

In memory of
Lawrence Berman CB
1928-2023
Virtus nescit labi

Copyright © The Old Stables Press

The right of Richard Berman to be identified as the author of this work has been asserted in accordance with the Copyright, Designs and Patents Act, 1988.

First published 2023 in the United Kingdom
The Old Stables Press, Goring Heath, Oxfordshire, RG8 7RT
theoldstablespress@gmail.com

All rights reserved. Except for the quotation of short passages for the purposes of criticism and review, no part of this publication may be reproduced, stored in a retrieval system, or transmitted in any form or by any means without the prior permission of the publisher.

All illustrations are copyright © Museum of Freemasonry, London, and used with their generous permission or are within the public domain. Cover image William Stewart, 1st Earl of Blessington (1709-1769); oil painting by Stephen Slaughter (1744) © Museum of Freemasonry, London.

British Library Cataloguing in Publication Data
A CIP catalogue record for this book is available from the British Library.

Library of Congress Cataloguing in Publication Data
Berman, Ric
The Second Grand Lodge. The Grand Lodge of Ireland, the London Irish & Antients Freemasonry
p. cm.
Includes biographical references.

ISBN 978-1-7391708-0-6

English – History - Modern
Irish – History - Modern
American – History - Modern

Other titles by Ric Berman

The Foundations of Modern Freemasonry –
The Grand Architects: Political Change and the
Scientific Enlightenment, 1714-1740

Schism: the Battle that Forged Freemasonry

Foundations - new light on the formation and early years of
The Grand Lodge of England
The 2016 Prestonian Lecture

Espionage, Diplomacy & the Lodge -
Charles Delafaye and the Secret Department of the Post Office

From Roanoke to Raleigh:
Freemasonry in North Carolina, 1730-1800

Loyalists & Malcontents:
Freemasonry & Revolution in South Carolina and Georgia

The Grand Lodge of England & Colonial America:
America's Grand Masters

Inventing the Future: The 1723 Constitutions

The 2024 Prestonian Lecture

May the road rise to meet you,
May the wind be always at your back.
May the sun shine warm upon your face,
The rains fall soft upon your fields.
And until we meet again,
May God hold you in the palm of his hand

Contents

	Page
Foreword	1
Introduction	3
The Grand Lodge of Ireland	14
The London Irish and Antients Freemasonry	24
The Aspirational London Irish	33
The Affluent London Irish	47
Antients Freemasonry in America	61
Meanwhile, back in Ireland	70
Laurence Dermott	87

Appendices

The Antients' Early Lodges	99
The First Antients' Lodges	100
Military Lodges	104
Military Warrants Issued by the Grand Lodge of Ireland	107
Military Warrants Issued by the Antients Grand Lodge	113
Overseas Lodges Warranted by the Grand Lodge of Ireland	115
The Prestonian Lecture – A History	123
Prestonian Lecturers, 1924-2024	126

'How shall I get through this world'
Eighteenth-century tavern sign

Foreword

Masonic lodges and freemasonry were present in Ireland before the Grand Lodge of Ireland was established in 1725. And while the Grand Lodge initially followed the pattern set out in London, it soon evolved, a function of economic, religious, social and political factors that were specific to Ireland. In terms of ritual and philosophical outlook, however, Irish freemasonry remained substantially analogous to its counterpart across the Irish Sea, a combination of fraternal sociability and eighteenth-century Enlightenment principles, not least religious tolerance, education and self-improvement.

As with English freemasonry, the impact of the Grand Lodge of Ireland and of Irish freemasonry extended beyond, indeed, far beyond the island of its birth. In Ireland's case this was articulated most plainly in the development of 'Antients' freemasonry, which was established by London's expatriate Irish community in the 1750s. This was a more socially inclusive and mutually supportive form of freemasonry that was not only shipped back to Ireland but, directly and indirectly, transported across Britain's burgeoning Empire, particularly North America, where it was carried by migration, trade and many regiments of the British Army.

It was also absorbed into mainstream English freemasonry following the union of the 'Moderns' – the first Grand Lodge of England – and the Antients, a merger that in 1813 created the United Grand Lodge of England.

The 2024 Prestonian Lecture recognises the seminal role that Antients and Irish freemasonry played in the widespread transmission of freemasonry and masonic and Enlightenment ideas across the globe. It also marks and celebrates the 2025 tercentenary of the Grand Lodge of Ireland.

The Second Grand Lodge rests on a combination of new research and older material, including *Schism: The battle that forged Freemasonry* (2013); *Antients Freemasonry and the London Irish*, a paper delivered in Dublin in 2014 to mark the centenary of the Irish Lodge of Research, No.CC; and *The Grand Lodge of England & Colonial America: America's Grand Masters* (2023).

Finally, and before we begin, I would like to thank the Trustees of the Prestonian Fund for the privilege of delivering the 2024 Prestonian Lecture in the centenary year of its re-establishment.

Ric Berman
South Oxfordshire

William Stewart, 1st Earl of Blessington
GM, Grand Lodge of Ireland, 1738-40; GM, Antients Grand Lodge, 1756-60

Introduction

I have been extremely fortunate to have spent considerable time - many pleasant months - in Ireland over the past several decades and to have witnessed how the country, and Dublin in particular, was fired by foreign investment and transformed into a 'Celtic tiger'. As Ireland's financial services and technology industries expanded vertiginously and economic growth outpaced almost every other country in Europe, incomes rose and Ireland gained a deeper sense of national pride and self-assurance. But alongside this self-confidence lay a curious lacuna: an almost intentional gap in Ireland's awareness of its early-modern history.

The Irish history syllabus offered (and still offers), two mutually exclusive areas for study: Early Modern (1492–1815) and Later Modern (1815–1993). In practice the vast majority of students pick the latter period and given the lack of modular flexibility, Early Modern is commonly ignored to the extent that for many it has become a largely unknown land.

The syllabus also divides between 'Ireland' and 'Europe and the wider world', with only limited attention devoted to the foundational aspects of England and Ireland's intertwined history and how that has impacted and continues to move political attitudes on both sides of the Irish Sea.

At this point I should emphasize that Irish history is also substantially absent from the British history syllabus. This is equally unfortunate and regrettable since mutual ignorance is not a sound basis for any relationship. For both countries, a failure to appreciate the substance, let alone the nuances, of England and Ireland's shared backstory from the fifteenth century onwards has raised a barrier to understanding that interconnected past. Indeed, many of the political and economic issues that dominate present-day Anglo-Irish and Anglo-Irish-American relations have roots in the sixteenth, seventeenth and eighteenth centuries which are as important as those that date to the centuries that followed.

Several factors underpin Ireland's preferred focus on nineteenth and twentieth-century history. It was during this period that Catholic emancipation was legislated into law with the Roman Catholic Relief Act of 1829, which repositioned the Catholic Church in Ireland as a potent force and helped to develop the country's independence movement. Social and political divisions and economic colonialism were also important influences, as was the difficult road to Independence itself.

This was a route that passed through the Home Rule debates of the 1870s and beyond, saw the 1916 Easter Rising, the Anglo-Irish War of 1919-21 and the treaty that followed, Ireland's partition and, eventually, the transformation of the Irish Free State into the Republic of Ireland.

But it was the devasting famines of 1845-52 and later years and the economic depression and destitution that accompanied them that have, perhaps, had the most profound impact upon Ireland at a political, emotional and almost visceral level. Those famines drove mass migration from the country on a scale so vast that it was carved deeply and indelibly into Ireland's psyche to the extent that it has become intrinsic to Irish and Irish-American self-perception and self-identity.

That is understandable. More than 4 million mainly Catholic Southern Irish left for the United States from the mid-1840s to the 1930s, sailing to Boston, New York and Philadelphia in particular. Many others crossed the Irish Sea to Britain to seek employment in the ports and factories of London, Liverpool, Birmingham, Glasgow and Manchester, or worked to build Britain's infrastructure – its canals, docks, factories and railways.

How this exodus impacted Ireland is documented in each decennial census. They record how the country's population peaked in 1841 at 8.18 million and then plunged, falling to 6.55 million in 1851, 5.18 million in 1881 and 4.46 million in 1901, at around which level it remained until the 1960s.

But this was not the only mass departure from Ireland and a focus on the nineteenth and twentieth centuries does not capture the entire story. Migration, mainly to America and Britain, also occurred in the eighteenth century. It was driven by successive famines in the 1740s when annual mortality reached 15-20%, a higher proportion of Ireland's population than in the Great Frost a century later. And it was a function of the repressive mercantilist trade and excise policies foisted on Ireland by London that led to a dearth of economic opportunity and stifled agricultural innovation and industrialization.

Although far less substantial in bare numbers when set against the millions in the years that followed, eighteenth-century migration was nonetheless significant. Around 400-450,000, and possibly more, left for North America and Britain between the 1730s and 1800. But this exodus was not dominated by Southern Irish Catholics but by Scots-Irish Presbyterians, Irish Quakers and other dissenting Protestants whose forebears had been encouraged to settle the 'plantations' of Munster and Ulster in the sixteenth and seventeenth centuries.

But to get to the point, despite many in Ireland and America believing that Ireland's independence movement began only in the late 1780s and 1790s with the Society of United Irishmen, Irish nationalism had raised its head many decades earlier. The movement was championed by Dublin's Protestant elites who embarked on what became an increasingly acrimonious political and economic debate with London.

In short, Ireland's road to independence was not a product of nineteenth and twentieth-century influences alone; there are broad and deep foundations in earlier centuries.

One of these rests on economics. Until the 1690s, Ireland was in several ways quite similar to and on a par with England. Although the Irish population was smaller, perhaps half that of England, both countries had roughly the same soil types and each benefitted (or suffered) from the same climate. Ireland and England also had broadly equivalent agricultural systems, raised the same livestock, grew many of the same crops, and both had extensive international trading relationships. And it was the last, from London's perspective, that gave rise to a problem. England suffered from a significant economic disadvantage when compared to Ireland: substantially higher labour costs. To give a key example, wool could be produced up to a third more cheaply in Ireland than in England.

It was this that led to sustained parliamentary lobbying by English merchants and landowners in favour of a trade policy that would reduce Irish competitiveness and tilt the market towards English agriculture and manufactures. The result was a run of highly discriminatory legislation beginning with the Wool Act of 1699, a law designed to protect English sheep farmers and woollen manufacturers from Irish (and colonial) competition: 'great quantities of... manufactures... [that] have of late been made and are daily increasing in the Kingdom of Ireland and in the English Plantations in America and are exported from thence to foreign market heretofore supplied from England which will inevitably sink the value of lands and tend to the ruin of the trade and woollen manufactures of this realm'.[1]

---

[1] 'An Act to prevent the Exportation of Wool out of the Kingdoms of Ireland and England into Foreign Parts and for the Encouragement of the Woollen Manufactures in the Kingdom of England': 11 Will III c.13 (1699). The text is from the preamble.

From Ireland's standpoint the legislation was financially disastrous and crashed the market once it became illegal for wool and woollen products to be exported from Ireland other than via England, where excise duties levied on import and re-export made Irish output uncompetitive.

The wool trade between Ireland and North America and the Caribbean plummeted and the price of Irish wool collapsed as overseas markets vanished. Irish farmers were driven to ruin and although production gradually shifted to linen exports which were free of excise duties, and there was widespread smuggling of Irish wool and woollen products, neither sufficed to restore agricultural incomes to the levels that had prevailed previously.

In England, Ireland's economic hardships were commonly ignored and attention focused instead on the cost and effectiveness of excise and naval enforcement, the London press, for example, noting the despatch of 'two frigates… to cruise the Irish coast in order to prevent the exportation of wool and the importation of contraband'.[2] Indeed, by the mid-1730s smuggling was recognised as a substantial problem and the number of naval vessels on station was increased accordingly with three men-of-war and eight armed sloops in Irish coastal waters 'to prevent the illegal exportation of wool and woollen goods to foreign parts'.[3]

London introduced further restrictions on Irish trade and manufacturing in the wake of the Wool Act, with laws regulating a raft of Irish enterprises from baking to meat-curing, butter-making, fishing and even street markets. Other regulations levied duties on almost all other Irish goods and merchandise and suppressed manufactured and agricultural products that were deemed to threaten their English counterparts. Only flax, hemp and linen were exempt.

Although driven principally by economic and financial self-interest, such laws were also fuelled by a widespread anti-Catholic sentiment in England and the fear that a competitive and thus financially robust Ireland would be more capable of providing effective support to the exiled James Stuart, the son of the former king, James II. Anti-Irish bigotry was generated by the English press in particular, which created and marketed a caricature of the Irish as violent, drunken and deeply unreliable rather than hard working, resilient and determined.

---

[2] *English Post Giving an Authentick Account of the Transactions of the World Foreign and Domestick*, 28-30 October 1700.

[3] *London Daily Post and General Advertiser*, 7 January 1736.

British political oppression reached another peak in 1720 with the passage of the Dependency of Ireland on Great Britain Act, which reversed the Irish Declaratory Act of 1689 which had confirmed that Ireland was a distinct kingdom, albeit under the same king. It was now the case that Ireland would be subordinate to Britain and that the king, via Parliament, had 'full power and authority to make laws and statutes to bind the kingdom and people of Ireland'.[4] Indeed, the Act went further, legislating that the Irish House of Lords no longer had jurisdiction to judge, affirm or reverse any judgment made in any court within Ireland, and that only the British House of Lords held such authority.

This was bad enough but Irish disaffection was reinforced by a crass decision in 1722 to allow William Wood, an English ironmaster, to coin Irish copper currency – something viewed in Ireland as an unlawful licence to mint money. Wood had bought the patent from the Duchess of Kendal, one of George I's mistresses, for £10,000, and there was a justifiable fear that he intended to debase Ireland's currency for his own profit.

Anglo-Irish opposition to Wood's patent ranged from the Church of Ireland to the Irish Parliament, but it was Jonathan Swift who roused the bulk of the country to resistance with his *Drapier's Letters*. Swift championed Irish nationalism, something assuaged, albeit only temporarily, by a tactical political retreat by Robert Walpole's administration in London.

The economic repression of Ireland continued nonetheless with the country ever more 'drained of money'.[5] London's orders obliged the Irish Treasury to fund not only the military and naval establishments in Ireland but also to co-finance regiments posted overseas. Irish taxes were, in addition, used to pay the salaries of absentee officers and fund an extended pension list, the bulk of which was given as patronage by the Crown to foreign recipients. And on top of this, rents paid to English owners of Irish land approached £1 million per year in a country where total output is estimated to have been less than £5 million.[6]

---

[4] 6. Geo. I c.5.

[5] William Connolly to the Duke of Grafton, 18 October 1720, quoted in Patrick Walsh, '"The Sin of With-Holding Tribute", contemporary pamphlets and the professionalisation of the Irish Revenue Service in the early eighteenth century', *Eighteenth-Century Ireland/Iris an dá chultúr*, 21 (2006), 48-65.

[6] A.P.W. Malcolmson, *Nathaniel Clements: Government & the Governing Elite in Ireland* (Dublin: Four Courts Press, 2005); Alice E. Murray, *A History of the Commercial &*

At the beginning of the eighteenth century virtually no-one within Ireland's Anglo-Irish elites leaned towards independence. English military protection was considered to be (and was) essential to the survival of Protestant minority rule and Ireland's Anglo-Irish were wholly supportive of George I and the Hanoverian line. The Protestant Hanoverians were perceived rightly as a political and military bulwark against the return of a potentially absolutist Catholic monarch in the form of the Pretender, James Stuart. But as the threat from Stuart and his Jacobite supporters receded, not least after the defeat of the 1745 Rising, the economic yoke imposed by London began to chafe more keenly and Britain's excise duties and its constraints on trade were recognised as ruinously oppressive.

Irish agriculture and manufacturing were shackled and exports depressed, and the country's economic woes were as predicted by the economist Charles Davenant five decades before: 'the price of land, value of rents, and our commodities and manufactures rise and fall, as it goes with our foreign trade'.[7]

For the majority of London's politicians and merchant traders this was not a problem. Regardless of complaints from otherwise loyal Anglo-Irish, until the almost the end of the eighteenth century, successive British governments viewed Ireland through a mercantilist lens as a subservient state: a colony, not a sister country. Although the two countries shared the same king, Ireland was not considered to be a truly sovereign nation nor deemed an economic or political equal while it remained under the protection of – and thus dependent upon - Britain's navy and army.

However, by the late 1750s, despite the waterfall of patronage and sinecures that lay at the heart of London's control of Ireland's parliament and the efficiency of Dublin's parliamentary managers or 'undertakers', Irish political opposition began to surge. Inflamed by London's condescension and driven by economic repression, Ireland's Protestant patriotic opposition voiced their concerns often and loudly and found a place at the forefront of Irish parliamentary debate until the Acts of Union in 1800 stifled dissent and pulled the political brake.

With not a little irony and over barely more than three generations, Britain's economic policies and political and social conceits pushed many

---

Financial Relations between England & Ireland from the Period of the Restoration (New York: Burt Franklin, 1970), reprint.

[7] Charles Davenant, *An Essay upon Ways and Means of Supplying the War* (London, 1695), p.82.

of its most loyal Irish supporters from one end of the political spectrum to the other: from firm advocates of dependency on England and promoters of Empire to staunch patriotic activists.

This would not have been the case had Ireland benefitted from true sovereignty and been accepted as a country with a political status equal to Britain. But it didn't and wasn't. And there were two principal reasons.

The first, a constitutional anachronism, was Poynings' Law, more formally Poynings' Act of 1495, which delegated control of Ireland's legislative process to England's Parliament. The law had been initiated by Sir Edward Poynings (1459-1521), the Lord Deputy of Ireland, and been approved by the Irish Parliament, ostensibly as a means of negating clan rivalries.

Poynings' Law limited Irish parliamentary power to approving or rejecting bills drawn up in London and made it unlawful for the Irish Parliament to be called without a license from the King of England. In short, no Irish law could take effect without English approval.

The second factor was English military repression.

England had maintained a strong interest in Ireland since at least 1173, when Henry II granted the right of residency in Dublin - *ad inhabitanda* - to the men of Bristol.

Henry VIII had declared himself king of Ireland in 1542. And Elizabeth I and James I (James VI of Scotland), reinforced England's control. They prosecuted a repressive colonial policy that was cemented by the 1594-1603 Nine Years' War in which an alliance of Irish chieftains and clans assisted by Spanish troops was routed by English forces.

The war came close to ruining England's finances and in an attempt to avoid future difficulties Ireland's clan leaders were offered clemency and the return of their lands in return for relinquishing their titles and arms and swearing loyalty to the English Crown. The offer was effectively rejected and in 1608 another rebellion emerged. It was suppressed at a near-prohibitive cost and English retribution followed swiftly with the confiscation of more Irish landholdings.

James I believed that increasing Protestant migration would buttress Crown authority in Ireland and reduce the risk of insurgency and in 1609 he established a Plantation in Ulster, seizing lands and granting title over them to Scottish and English settlers or 'planters'. It was by this means that Ulster came to be dominated by Scots-Presbyterians who continued to arrive in large numbers through to the 1690s.

James's policy was similar to that of Elizabeth I who had created a Plantation in Munster settled by English Protestants as retribution for the 'Desmond Rebellions' of 1569-73 and 1579-83. Those uprisings had been put down viciously and the Earldom of Desmond's three-century dominance of south-west Ireland was terminated as a result.

In 1641 another Irish-Catholic rebellion against English and Scots-Irish hegemony triggered the Eleven Years' War, also known as the 'Confederate Wars'. That uprising was halted by Oliver Cromwell's New Model Army which invaded in 1649 and undertook a four-year scorched-earth campaign. An estimated 200,000 people were killed, possibly more. The number would be large in any context but was especially so given Ireland's then population of around 1-2 million.

The punitive sanctions that followed reinforced English and Scottish ascendancy over Ireland and were accompanied by further confiscations and retitling of Irish estates to compensate Cromwell's officers and soldiers for their military service. Many defeated Irish insurgents were sent overseas to work as indentured labour, not least in the Caribbean sugar colonies. Others were executed, imprisoned or fled.

The uneasy Anglo-Irish peace that followed was not negotiated but imposed. It laid the foundations for another two centuries of involuntary Irish-Catholic submission, political and religious.

The transfer of physical land and assets from Catholics to Protestants was accompanied by the conveyance of political control. A discriminatory anti-Catholic legal code, the 'penal laws', was introduced and applied with rigor. The code would remain substantially in place throughout the eighteenth century with the final restrictions removed only in 1829.

Opposition to English rule was not razed by Cromwell but forced to the margins and underground. The dismissal of James II from the English, Scottish and Irish thrones in 1688 and the 'Glorious Revolution' that replaced him with the Protestant duo of William and Mary triggered an uprising among James II's supporters in Ireland. Their aim was to turn the country into a Catholic base from which James could launch a campaign to return to power and regain his thrones. But the plan failed. James's Irish army was eviscerated at the Battle of the Boyne in 1690 and buried at the Battle of Aughrim the following year. Irish Jacobitism and Irish-Catholic nationalism were damaged so badly that not even the Jacobite Risings of 1715 and 1745 in which Scotland and Northern England rebelled against the Hanoverians George I and George II, respectively, triggered support for the Stuart cause in Ireland, let alone fomented an effective rebellion.

Despite this, Irish-Catholic opposition to British rule remained, sustained in part by the expatriate Irish displaced to continental Europe, including those in attendance at the Stuarts' exiled Court at Avignon and then Rome.

The 1691 Treaty of Limerick that ended the Williamite Wars in Ireland had allowed Irish combatants to seek exile in France. Known as the 'Flight of the Wild Geese', an estimated 20,000 Irish combatants departed, many to serve in Louis XIV's Irish Brigades.[8] Irish expatriates also joined other European armies, including Spain's, which mustered five Irish regiments, and Austria's, where the Irish were deployed across Eastern and Central Europe. Irish soldiers were also present in the Swedish, Polish and Russian armies, Milan's Spanish Army, and Sicily's Limerick Regiment.

The migration of potentially rebellious Catholic men and their recruitment for military service in Europe was tacitly and sometimes actively encouraged by England. Indeed, initially the flight was seen as potentially advantageous – at least in the short term – in that it removed a latent threat to Ireland's domestic stability. Estimates vary but over the half century from 1691-1745, when foreign military recruitment in Ireland was finally prohibited, around 200,000 Irishmen are thought to have left to serve in Europe's armies.

Perhaps ironically, the Irish also served, often with distinction, in the British army and navy. A large number volunteered as a way out of poverty, others were impressed, something encouraged by the Irish Parliament which passed enabling legislation. And although desertion was a constant problem, during the eighteenth century around a third of the ranks in Britain's armed forces were Irish.

Throughout the eighteenth-century the island of Ireland was a Protestant hegemony with the country's penal laws deployed to maintain the dominance of the Anglican Church of Ireland minority. Catholics and Protestant Dissenters, together more than 80% of the population, were disenfranchised and in 1728 even Catholic peers who had taken a loyal oath of allegiance were barred from sitting in the Irish House of Lords.

---

[8] Following the Treat of Ryswick in 1697, France disbanded a number of regiments, including the Irish, who were ordered to leave France within six weeks 'upon pain of being hang'd as deserted soldiers': *Post Boy*, 30 December 1699 - 2 January 1700.

Other sanctions controlled more middling Catholics, with regulations that excluded them from many professions as well as the judiciary. Catholic access to education in Ireland was also curbed, with Catholics banned from attending public schools and from matriculating at Trinity College, Dublin, then Ireland's sole university.

Such restrictions were not unique in Europe and should be seen in the context of 250 years of post-Reformation religious warfare. In particular, they mirrored the constraints imposed on French Protestants – Huguenots – by Louis XIII, XIV and XV, as did the ban on inter-marriage between Protestants and Catholics. Indeed, French legislation may have provided the model on which Ireland's penal laws were based. In short, the legal discrimination against Irish Catholics had a strong parallel to that wielded against Protestants in continental Europe.

The Reformation had begun in Germany in the second decade of the sixteenth century, spread rapidly, and was soon viewed as synonymous with opposition to the established religious and political order. Across Europe, but especially in France, the authorities responded with arrests, imprisonment and executions, with deemed heretics driven into exile. Their number included John Calvin, who fled to Basel, then Geneva, before moving to Strasbourg.

Nonetheless, a Calvinist church was founded in Paris a decade later and notwithstanding harassment by the Catholic Church, Calvinism expanded. Growth brought the movement into conflict with the Catholic aristocracy and church hierarchy, whose power it threatened. And the reaction was forceful.

The Duke of Guise, a senior French aristocrat, sanctioned an attack on a Calvinist - Huguenot - congregation at Vassy in March 1562. It foreshadowed what would be more than two centuries of violent religious conflict, something encapsulated by the St Bartholomew's Day Massacre a decade later in August 1572 when mob violence against the Huguenot community rippled out from Paris to cities and towns across France. Estimates of the number of Protestants killed over the weeks that followed vary, but the estimates run from the low tens of thousands to 70-80,000, with at least one exceeding the upper band.

The Catholic hierarchy regarded the carnage as having secured deliverance from heresy and France from a conspiracy to overturn the state. Protestant countries in Europe were aghast and reports of the massacre by Sir Francis Walsingham, Elizabeth I's ambassador to France, did much to reinforce England's anti-Catholic and pro-Huguenot political stance.

Huguenot persecution continued in France regardless, with many tens of thousands forcibly converted to Catholicism. Those who refused faced the confiscation of their assets and sanctions that included imprisonment. And in the 1680s, Protestant maltreatment reached an apogee under Louis XIV with the forced billeting of French dragoons on Huguenot households: the 'Dragonnades'. The policy was synonymous with violence, rape and theft. Louis XIV also rescinded the limited protections that his grandfather, Henry IV, had offered the Huguenots under the Edict of Nantes, depriving them of their remaining civil and religious liberties.

Huguenot migration from France accelerated in response. A trickle became a torrent and, despite the risks, an estimated third of France's remaining Protestants fled, around 250,000 people, with more leaving in later years.

But to return to Ireland. Notwithstanding the country's *de jure* anti-Catholic penal laws (and unlike France), there was *de facto* pragmatism. Ireland's Catholic gentry were permitted to send their sons to be educated in continental Europe and inter-faith marriages took place, albeit in England rather than in Ireland. And while Catholics were generally prevented from possessing arms, exceptions were made for 'papist gentlemen who can prove themselves comprised under the Articles of Limerick' who were allowed to hold 'swords, pistols and guns... to defend their house or for fowling'.

Aristocratic and even middling Catholic families ensured that at least one son converted to Protestantism, even if this were in name only, to preserve family estates and influence.[9] Catholic worship continued, albeit that priests were required to be approved and registered. And Irish culture survived, mainly in the west and north-west of Ireland, although the Gaelic that had been spoken by the majority of the population in the seventeenth century was gradually replaced by English.

---

[9] To a lesser extent the same occurred in France, with the eldest son in some aristocratic Huguenot families converting to Catholicism in order to avoid the loss of the family estates.

The Grand Lodge of Ireland

The introduction to Dublin and Cork of the English model of modern freemasonry lagged developments in London by around five years. The starting point was almost certainly the Duke of Montagu's decision to accept the position of grand master of the Grand Lodge of England, something which attracted considerable interest in Ireland. Montagu, one of Britain and Ireland's wealthiest and best-known celebrity aristocrats, demonstrated that freemasonry was acceptable morally, intellectually and politically – and that it could be fashionable as well as fun.

The combination provided the rationale for those of 'the best rank' and for 'learned scholars of most professions and denominations' to establish or join a masonic lodge. Many others followed. And it was from this point that freemasonry featured in many if not most of Dublin's newspapers and became an accepted part of the city's social life.

John Whalley's *Dublin News Letter* carried a description of Montagu's installation in July 1721 and the following month John Harding's opposition-leaning *Dublin Impartial News Letter* recorded the initiation of a slew of aristocrats and political figures at the King's Arms Tavern in St Paul's Churchyard.

The Duke of Wharton's decision to join the Craft similarly drew attention, with Ireland's newspapers alerting their readers to 'his Grace [having been] admitted into the Society of Freemasons'. Wharton became grand master of the Grand Lodge of England in succession to Montagu in 1722.

Despite having sold most of his Irish estates to invest in South Sea stock, a decision which proved to be a financial catastrophe and cost much of his fortune, Wharton retained many friends within the Anglo-Irish elites where he had inherited the titles of Marquess of Catherlough, Earl of Rathfarnam and Baron Trim in the Irish peerage, alongside his English titles. His inner circle included Richard Parsons, the 1st Earl of Rosse, who would in just a few short years become the first grand master of the Grand Lodge of Ireland.

Born in 1702 in Twickenham to the west of London, Rosse had succeeded to his father's viscountcy as a child and at the age of 22 was raised to an earldom in the Irish peerage as an encouragement to maintain his pro-Hanoverian loyalty. Equally importantly, and in common with Wharton, Rosse was a fashionable social figure.

Philip, Duke of Wharton
Marquess of Catherlough, Earl of Rathfarnam and Baron Trim
in the Irish peerage
Grand Master, Grand Lodge of England, 1722

The Earl of Rosse was installed as grand master of Ireland in 1725 and may have remained the titular head of Irish freemasonry until 1731, when he departed on a Grand Tour of Europe and Egypt.

He was succeeded by James King, 4th Lord Kingston, a former grand master of the Grand Lodge of England (1728-9). Indeed, there were strong connections between the two grand lodges from the 1720s to the 1740s.

Rosse had rank, celebrity and an extensive social network in Ireland where the family had had a presence and estates for some two centuries. He was young, affluent and politically loyal, as were his grand officers. And as with the Duke of Montagu, Rosse served as beacon to attract others from his social circle and beyond into freemasonry.

A number of historians have argued that in its formative years the Grand Lodge of Ireland was subject to a factional struggle between Irish Jacobites and pro-Hanoverian Whigs, and that Irish freemasonry was split accordingly. It is possible that Rosse's friendship with the Jacobite Duke of Wharton is at the root of this belief. Both men founded or joined Hell Fire Clubs, Wharton in London and Rosse in Dublin. And both were somewhat mercurial young adults with a common interest in gambling, drinking, whoring and mischief-making. Indeed, William Chetwode Crawley, a masonic historian, describes Rosse as a man whose 'ideas of morals were inverted' and whose 'skill shone most in the management of the small-sword and the dice-box'.

But whether that is correct or otherwise, Rosse, unlike Wharton, was attuned to the prevalent political mood. And notwithstanding his libertinism, something not uncommon among the aristocracy and gentry in Dublin and London, he was loyal to the Hanoverian line, as were his officers: the Hon. Humphrey Butler, his deputy; Sir Thomas Prendergast, his senior grand warden, a first cousin to the Duke of Richmond's wife, Lady Sarah Cadogan; Marcus Anthony Morgan, the junior grand warden; and Thomas Griffiths, grand secretary.

Taken as a whole, there is no substantive evidence that the Grand Lodge of Ireland was the subject of a struggle for political influence or dominance as between Irish Jacobites and pro-Hanoverian Whigs, nor that Irish freemasonry was divided. The opposite was the case, with Irish freemasonry reflecting the political ascendancy of the pro-Hanoverian elites. And although the political flavour of Ireland's Grand Lodge changed over time and became antipathetic to Britain and British establishment interests, this was not a function of an anti-Hanoverian or pro-Jacobite political shift, or republicanism, but a reaction to the British government's imposition of increasingly harsh and self-serving trade policies, and a response to London's overt social and political disparagement.

The main motive behind the creation of the Grand Lodge of Ireland and the participation of Dublin's aristocrats, gentry and professional classes was a desire to emulate the splendour and renown of the Grand Lodge of England and to identify with the Enlightenment philosophy and Newtonian science with which freemasonry was associated. Engagement with such concepts was also expressed elsewhere, not least in the formation of the Dublin Society which promoted national improvement through the application of scientific method and the encouragement of the arts.

The Dublin press published regular articles on freemasonry throughout the 1720s, including popular exposés such as *The Grand Mystery of the Free-Masons Disclosed*, and the riposte, *The Free-Masons Vindication, being an Answer to a Scandalous Libel*. At the same time, the 1723 Constitutions were advertised widely and made available for purchase from Dublin's many booksellers.

The first press report of a meeting of the Grand Lodge of Ireland appears in June 1725 in *The Dublin Weekly Journal*, which set out a detailed account of Rosse's appointment as grand master. Covering almost a full page, the article describes the procession, installation and subsequent grand feast, recording that more than a hundred gentlemen met at the Yellow Lion tavern in Warborough Street and 'after some time putting on their aprons, white gloves and other parts of the distinguishing dress of that Worshipful Order… proceeded over Essex bridge to the Strand and from thence to the King's Inns'.

The parade comprised the masters and wardens of 'six lodges of gentleman freemasons… under the jurisdiction of the Grand Master', and after 'marching round the walls of the great hall… the grand lodge, composed of the Grand Master… Grand Wardens and the masters and wardens of the lodges, retired to the room prepared for them where… they proceeded to the election of a new Grand Master'. The article continues, noting that they afterwards 'went to [a] play, with their aprons etc., the private brothers sat in the pit, but the Grand Master, Deputy Grand Master and Grand Wardens, in the government's box'.

The article was written in a style that implied that the Grand Lodge of Ireland had been in existence for some time, thus playing to the notions of longevity and substance. However, there is little doubt that the Grand Lodge of Ireland was a more recent construct.

Interestingly, although modelled on the Grand Lodge of England, there were points of difference between the two organisations even in 1725, perhaps most notably the election of grand officers by the members of Grand Lodge as a whole. In England, such officers were appointed by the grand master.

In 1730 John Pennell, later grand secretary of the Grand Lodge of Ireland, published the first Irish version of the 1723 Constitutions. He had advertised in George Faulkner's *Dublin Journal* for a minimum of two hundred subscribers and achieved that objective without difficulty. His Constitutions contain a small number of variations in ritual, including the prayer at initiation and the responsibilities of the deacons, a role undertaken largely by stewards in England. However, over time and for reasons that were more socio-political than masonic, these and other variations came to be perceived as more substantive.

Another edition of the Irish Constitutions was published in 1751 by Edward Spratt, then grand secretary of the Grand Lodge of Ireland. In his dedication to Lord Kingsborough, the grand master, Spratt makes the point that he should not be considered the author but 'editor and transcriber', writing that authorship should be ascribed to the 'learned and ingenious brother, James Anderson'. Spratt also underlined that there were no essential differences in his volume as compared to the original 1723 Constitutions, bar the absence of 'those Rules that tended to the Steward's [sic] Lodge' since Ireland had no such lodge, 'a thing not practised here'.

This rather puts to rest the contention that the masonic rift that developed between London and Dublin in the second half of the eighteenth century was due solely to differences in ritual. Indeed, the roots of the split lie in the creation of the expatriate-Irish-led, London-based 'Antients Grand Lodge', formed in 1751, and to a growing antagonism driven by political, social and economic hostility.

Although the masonic relationship between the Grand Lodge of Ireland and the Grand Lodge of England was restored in 1813 with the creation of the United Grand Lodge of England that brought together the Antients and Moderns, Antients freemasonry's masonic influence endured. In particular, the Antients magnified Irish freemasonry's greater social inclusivity and expanded greatly the number of those who could and would become freemasons. And this was not only the case in Ireland but also in England and internationally, and especially in North America.

An important part of this process was the publication in 1756 of Laurence Dermott, the Antients' grand secretary's *Ahiman Rezon*, the Antients' book of constitutions, which displaced the 1723 Constitutions in both Antients and Irish lodges, albeit that it was based almost wholly on Spratt's Irish Constitutions and thus on the original 1723 Constitutions.

Dermott promoted Antients freemasonry in three main ways. First, by opening up the organisation to a wider membership. Second, by ushering in compulsory, as opposed to voluntary, charitable contributions, thereby creating a proto-friendly society. And third and most controversially, by denigrating the original premier Grand Lodge of England as 'Moderns', a term that was and was designed to be pejorative.

The Irish and Antients grand lodges also innovated in several areas. This included the issuance of travelling warrants, not least to British regiments transiting through Ireland to America, the Caribbean and elsewhere, a move that helped to spread freemasonry across the globe. And it encompassed the provision of certificates to members in good standing, providing such members with what quickly became a masonic passport that allowed them to access masonic support groups in lodges and communities nationally and overseas where they would otherwise have been unknown.

Lodge membership registers, the lists of subscribers to masonic books and periodicals, and contemporary press reports, all point to how Irish and Antients freemasonry altered over time. From an exclusive and mainly Protestant organisation in the 1730s, it adapted to become far more socially inclusive and almost fully inter-denominational with an increasingly substantial number of Catholic members.

Several factors drove the process. As in England, one motive for joining a masonic lodge was the forum that freemasonry provided for local association. An invitation to fraternal drinking and dining was attractive as an end in itself but this was enhanced by the additional potential benefits of networking. Freemasonry's tolerance of different religions was another key factor and something especially important in Ireland, where the lodge brought together Protestants, Catholics and Quakers.

The spirituality of a quasi-religious ritual would also have held appeal, again something of particular significance in Ireland where Catholic worship was circumscribed and non-conformist religion discouraged. And there were other influences. Fraternal benevolence did not equate only to giving charity, it included its receipt. Complete financial security may not have been on offer but lodge funds were available to assist distressed members and their families, not least following a death or during periods of illness or unemployment.

The importance of this aspect of Irish and Antients freemasonry was reflected at the time in the weight attached to masonic funerals, something underlined by the prominence given to such events by the Irish press. A similar approach was taken by the Antients in England:

> *That upon the death of any of our worthy brethren whose names are or may be hereafter recorded in the Grand Registry &c., the Master of such lodge as he then belonged to shall immediately inform the Grand Secretary of his death and the intended time for his funeral, and upon this notice the Grand Secretary shall summon all the lodges to attend the funeral in proper order, and that each member shall pay one shilling towards defraying the expenses of said funeral or otherwise to his widow or nearest friend.*[10]

In Ireland as in England, the patronage of members of the aristocracy provided political cover for freemasonry which was in both countries far from being a secret society. Indeed, the pomp and ceremony of masonic parades, dinners, dances and other entertainments may have been a far more effective draw than any supposedly secret signs and tokens that were communicated privately in the lodge.

Processions accompanied by music - and in port towns naval salutes - with members in full regalia, often ended with public church services celebrating the semi-annual St John's Days or the laying of civic foundation stones. Other masonic events included dances and theatrical evenings, where concerts and plays were preceded and followed by masonic verse and song; and even masonically-themed horse racing.

Such events occurred regularly, not only in Dublin but also across Irish towns and cities more widely:

> *By Command of the Right Worshipful and Rt Hon Ford, Earl of Cavan, Grand Master of Ireland. For the benefit of distressed Free and accepted Masons.*

---

[10] Antients Grand Lodge *Minutes*, 1 July 1752.

On Thursday the 22nd of June, will be a Grand Concert of vocal and instrumental music. The Grand Master, with the Grand Officers and brethren, will appear in their jewels and proper clothing, according to ancient customs; [Ranelagh Gardens] will be illuminated, and a large additional band of music provided to attend the grand procession round the gardens.[11]

Loughrea [Co. Galway], June 25th, 1755. Yesterday being St John's Day, the Patron Saint of the Most Antient and Honourable Fraternity of Free and Accepted Masons, the Free Masons of this Town, of lodge No.248, met at some distance from the town from whence they marched in procession preceded by a band of music to the Fountain Tavern where they dined, and after dinner drank all the toasts peculiar to Masonry, the Royal Family, the Glorious Pious and Immortal Memory of King William, and other loyal toasts. At six in the evening, they marched to the Assembly Rooms where they gave an elegant Ball to the Ladies and Gentlemen. The Ball was opened by the Master; the first set consisted of twenty couple, the Men all Masons, and the Ladies (to do honour to the Fraternity), wore blue ribbons, and particularly a blue rose on each of their left breasts.[12]

At the dinner that followed, Loughrea lodge 'agreed unanimously to subscribe for a prize of fifty guineas, to be run for next August, at the course of Loughrea, by four-year-old horses, etc., the property of Freemasons of any regular lodge whatsoever'.[13]

Unlike most other clubs, societies and institutions in Ireland, freemasonry offered a bridge that crossed the divide between social ranks and religious denominations. And as the eighteenth century progressed this became ever more obvious. By the 1790s, Irish freemasonry had expanded to include urban and rural lodges whose members spanned the social spectrum from landed gentry to the Protestant and Catholic working class. This is not to argue that every Irish lodge was open to everyone. Class remained socially divisive and lodge fees and expenses for admission, dress, dining and the annual levy and compulsory charitable contributions were used as *de facto* barriers to exclude or discourage those deemed unsuitable. There is also evidence that religious discrimination had not been erased across the board. Nonetheless, Irish freemasonry was considerably less

---

[11] *Dublin Mercury*, 17-20 June 1769.
[12] *Dublin Gazette*, 24-28 June 1755; *Faulkner's Dublin Journal*, 28 June - 2 July 1757.
[13] *Pue's Occurrences*, 25-28 June 1757.

socially stratified than elsewhere in Europe and, probably for this reason, by the 1790s had become by far the most popular form of civil association in Ireland.

Petri Mirala's comparative analysis of European freemasonry suggests that in relation to its population, Irish freemasonry had a larger footprint than in any other European country with almost four times as many members in proportion to its population as compared to England.[14] Some 700 lodges were warranted in Ireland between 1730 and 1790, aggregating to around 40,000 or more members in an adult male population of 1-2 million. The comparable numbers for England are 20-25,000 masons in an adult male population of 2-3 million. This is comparable to France with some 40-50,000 masons in an adult male population of $c.$7-8 million.

Most Irish lodges guarded their independence jealously, especially those based some distance from Dublin and outside the immediate orbit of the Grand Lodge of Ireland. Consequently, early attempts by Dublin to impose a federal structure over its notionally subordinate lodges failed. As Lisa Meaney notes in her study of Munster freemasonry, the lodges resented interference, and sometimes aggressively so.[15]

Fifty-eight lodges were warranted in Munster from 1726 to 1760. Co. Cork had twenty-two lodges; Limerick and Waterford, ten each; Tipperary, nine; and Clare and Kerry, one apiece. Several probably pre-dated the establishment of the Grand Lodge of Ireland in 1725 but even after the mid-1730s when the Grand Lodge of Ireland was fully operational there is little evidence of anything other than a fragile relationship between Dublin and outlying lodges. An instructive incident was the attempt in May 1748 by John Calder, the grand secretary, to compile a report on the condition of Munster's lodges and collect outstanding lodge dues. It was – and was viewed as – an attempt by Dublin to exert its authority, however, Calder's report suggests that this was virtually non-existent. One Munster lodge stated that it would 'never pay any dues, except a shilling from each Master and sixpence from each Warden, on the commencement of their officers and secretary's fees for registry'.[16]

---

[14] Petri Mirala, *Freemasonry in Ulster, 1733-1813: A Social and Political History of the Masonic Brotherhood in the North of Ireland* (Dublin: Four Courts Press, 2007); & 'Masonic sociability and its limitations', in James Kelly, Martyn J. Powell (eds), *Clubs and Societies in Eighteenth-Century Ireland* (Dublin: Four Courts Press, 2010).

[15] Lisa Meaney, *Freemasonry in Munster, 1726-1829* (Mary Immaculate College, 2005).

In the event, an informal accommodation was reached whereby the grand lodge chose to ignore most provincial irregularities and the majority of their dues went unremitted.

That a growing number of Irish Catholics joined freemasonry from the mid-eighteenth century onwards is apparent from the membership registers of individual lodges with the rise predating by decades Catholic emancipation in Ireland. Of course, Catholic freemasons were not present uniformly across Ireland and not all lodges were inter-denominational. And although a few lodges continued to exclude Catholics either formally or less formally, many were open to both Catholics and Protestants and the masonic practice of 'inter-visitation', visiting other local lodges, expanded social as well as masonic contacts across the divide.

Given the formal attitude of the Catholic Church towards freemasonry, it is important to underline that the papal bulls of 1738 and 1751 and canon law against freemasonry were more-or-less ignored in Ireland in the eighteenth century.[17]

One reason can be found in the changes that took place following Catholic emancipation in the late 1820s. Before then Catholicism had been constrained by legislation and the imposition of strict papal doctrine on freemasonry would probably have been detrimental to the Catholic Church's emergence from sanction. Moreover, the masonic lodge was one of few forums where men of different denominations and faiths could meet.

But this ignores another point: freemasonry genuinely appealed to Irish Catholics. Many priests became freemasons as did several bishops, and in 1788 Ireland's archbishops petitioned Pope Pius VI to argue that the penalty of automatic excommunication should be withdrawn.[18] Indeed, the popularity of freemasonry across Ireland's religious divide grew and by the 1790s it was seen widely as a non-sectarian organisation.

The rationale behind Rome's attempts to undermine freemasonry had been and continued to be political. By promoting religious tolerance, self-improvement, scientific education, constitutionalism and meritocracy, freemasonry undermined traditional Catholic doctrine and threatened its symbiotic relationship with Europe's 'divinely-anointed' autocratic

---

[16] John Heron Lepper & Philip Crossle, *History of the Grand Lodge of Free and Accepted Masons of Ireland* (Dublin: Lodge of Research, CC, 1925), vol. I, pp.113-4.

[17] The same was true elsewhere in Catholic Europe, including several Italian states.

[18] Mirala, *Freemasonry in Ulster*, pp.135-6. Also, *Irish Clubs and Societies*, pp.327-8.

monarchies. It also posed a material threat to the spiritual authority and primary function of the Catholic Church as the sole portal to heaven.

Rome denounced freemasons as heretics who should be opposed with excommunication and the Inquisition. But it was a stance that failed to be shared widely and over time freemasonry grew in popularity to the extent that by the end of the eighteenth century the lodge held a position at the heart of polite sociability. Regardless, in the wake of the Roman Catholic Relief Act which shattered Anglican supremacy in Ireland, Leo XII's 1826 papal Bull against secret societies was promulgated extensively and Catholic freemasons were threatened with excommunication if they failed to resign.

The London Irish & Antients Freemasonry

If one were to identify a single point at which London's Irish community began to veer away from English freemasonry it would be 11 December 1735. On that day, the Grand Lodge of England met at the Devil Tavern, Temple Bar, London. Three senior grand officers were absent and in their places George Payne was 'desired to take the Chair as Grand Master' and 'Bro. Lambell and Dr Anderson... took their seats as Grand Wardens pro tempore'. Martin Clare, the junior grand warden, stepped up to sit as deputy grand master.

After opening Grand Lodge and reading the minutes of the last Quarterly Communication and Charity Committee, the minutes record

> Notice being given to the Grand Lodge that the Master and Wardens of a lodge from Ireland attended without desiring to be admitted by virtue of a Deputation from the Lord Kingston, present Grand Master of Ireland. But it appearing there was no particular recommendation from his Lordship in this affair, their Request could not be complied with, unless they would accept of a new Constitution here.[19]

James King, Lord Kingston, had served as grand master of English Grand Lodge in 1729 and in 1735 was sitting for the second time as grand master of the Grand Lodge of Ireland. Given his distinction it may have been reasonable to expect that a deputation in his name would have been

---

[19] Grand Lodge of England *Minutes*, 1723-39, pp.259-60.

welcomed. However, with the apparent excuse that 'there was no particular recommendation from his Lordship', the Irish were snubbed and their request to be admitted 'could not be complied with'. The event stands out and on the surface appears to run against the fraternal philosophy that freemasonry professes to follow.

William Songhurst, a former master of Quatuor Coronati Lodge and editor of *Ars Quatuor Coronatorum* ('AQC'), the *Transactions* of the Lodge, attempted to explain the rebuff by noting 'the absence of fraternal intercourse' between the Antients and Moderns and commenting that the decision to reject the Irish delegation 'seems to point to alterations having been made which prevented inter-visitation':

> *We know that the premier Grand Lodge was not recognised either in Ireland or Scotland, though both maintained fraternal correspondence with the Antients. Recognition by the Grand Lodges in the sister kingdoms, and a union with the Grand Lodge of the Antients only became possible after the resolution passed by the Moderns in 1809 "that it is not necessary any longer to continue in force those measures which were resorted to in or about the year 1739 respecting irregular masons, and do therefore enjoin the several lodges to revert to the ancient land marks of the Society".*

Songhurst is wrong, and demonstrably so. First and most obviously, the Antients Grand Lodge did not come into being until 1751 (initially as a 'Grand Committee'), sixteen years after the event under discussion. Second, the formal schism between the grand lodges of Ireland and England did not occur until 1758, when Ireland broke off fraternal correspondence with the Moderns and recognised the Antients in its place, a decision that followed William Stewart, 1st Earl of Blessington's agreement in 1756 to serve as the Antients' first noble grand master. (Blessington, a leading Irish aristocrat, had been Ireland's grand master from 1738-39.) And third, the Grand Lodge of Scotland did not recognise the Antients until 1773, when the 3rd Duke of Atholl was simultaneously grand master of the Antients and grand master-elect of the Grand Lodge of Scotland. At that point Scotland entered into a formal pact with Ireland under which both grand lodges recognised the Antients to the exclusion of the original Grand Lodge of England.

Songhurst is also wrong on a second count: that 'alterations [had] been made [to masonic ritual] which prevented inter-visitation'. There were, broadly, two relevant sets of changes. First, in the 1720s, when Desaguliers, Payne and others at the Grand Lodge of England had modernised lodge ritual, adopting an Enlightenment approach to promote religious tolerance and self-improvement via education. But this had not prevented inter-visitation or made freemasonry less popular; it had had the opposite effect. Under the auspices of the Grand Lodge of England with its reworked charges and regulations, freemasonry grew rapidly in terms of grass roots membership and with respect to the number of lodges accepting the authority of the new grand lodge.[20] However, although it is possible that Songhurst was referring to these earlier alterations, it is more probable that he was writing of other changes that took place in the late 1730s, three or four years after the date on which the Irish deputation had been barred from admission.

This second set of amendments has been identified by Songhurst and others as being at the centre of the dispute between the Antients and Moderns. And given its role as the supposed principal *casus belli* that initiated and sustained six decades of acrimony between the two organisations, it is appropriate to examine the issue in detail.[21]

The adoption by the Moderns of what the Antients criticised as 'innovative ritual' was termed 'the discard... of the old unwritten traditions of the Order'. Hence, there are two questions: did such changes occur; and, if so, how extensive and comprehensive were they. The answer to the first question is 'yes'. Why else would the Moderns have resolved in 1809 that it was no longer necessary for them to continue 'those measures which were resorted to in or about the year 1739'. However, the answer to the second point is harder to clarify. Although the ritual used by Irish and Antients freemasons *was* at variance with that used by what was self-termed 'regular' English freemasonry, the nature and extent of the divergence needs to be understood both in absolute terms and in context.

A key point is that the changes made in the late 1730s were considerably *less* far-reaching than is often supposed. In the eighteenth century, masonic ritual took different forms in each of England, Ireland and Scotland. But masonic practices also varied regionally, as well as from town-to-town and lodge-to-lodge. This was a function of an oral

---

[20] Cf., Ric Berman, *Foundations of Modern Freemasonry* (Brighton: Sussex Academic Press, 2011, 2nd edn 2014).

[21] Lepper & Crossle, *History of the Grand Lodge of Ireland*, vol. I, p.232.

tradition that tended to frustrate homogeneity, something achieved only later and then only in part when different versions of masonic ritual were 'approved' and committed to paper. It was also customary practice that individual lodges determined for themselves the nature of the ritual they followed and this remains the case, at least in English lodges, where there are some fourteen forms of accepted masonic ritual, each of which has distinctive characteristics to a greater or lesser extent.

Turning to the specifics of the ritual-based accusations levied at the Moderns, the most frequent Antients complaint was that 'in or about 1739' the traditional passwords and handshakes that comprised the accepted form of masonic recognition in the first and second-degree ceremonies were transposed. The switch had supposedly been made at the suggestion of the Grand Lodge of England to exclude freemasons whose knowledge had been gleaned from the press rather than from participating in a lodge. However, such a ruse would have become known rapidly. An alternative and more probable explanation is that such changes were introduced as an excuse to bar those believed to be of insufficient social standing. This is discussed in more detail below.

Other Irish and Antients' criticism was directed at what was viewed as the Moderns' over-secularisation of freemasonry, especially in the omission of religious symbolism, changes to the way in which initiates were prepared, a failure to recite the Old Charges in full (a quite lengthy process), and omitting to use swords in the initiation ceremony. Further objections were directed at the use of 'stewards' to undertake roles performed in Ireland by 'deacons'; and, perhaps most tellingly, that the Moderns did not permit additional degrees to be worked in the lodge.

A few complaints were relatively minor or even specious, and virtually all were undermined by the reality that eighteenth-century masonic ritual varied widely with differences the rule rather than an exception. But in most areas of substance the ritual used by the Moderns and Antients was aligned. Confirmation of this was provided at the time in *Hiram: or the Grand Master Key*, published in 1766, which compares the two rituals and confirms the extent to which they overlapped and the absence of material contradictions.[22] This should not be surprising. There is only modest evidence that points to differences in ritual as the primary

---

[22] Anonymous, *Hiram: or the Grand Master Key* (London: W. Griffin, 1766), 2nd edn.

motive for the creation of Antients freemasonry and the root cause of the later schism. But if ritual was not the central driver, what was…

The work of two Victorian historians, Robert Freke Gould and Henry Sadler, underpins the received explanation of the dispute between the Antients and Moderns and how the Antients Grand Lodge came to be established.[23] Gould's synopsis is based substantially on the minutes of what he dismissively called 'that schismatic body, commonly, but erroneously, termed the *Antient Masons*' and is limited to an analysis of freemasonry itself. Anecdotally, and despite his partiality against the 'schismatics', Gould was quite appreciative of the effectiveness of Laurence Dermott, the Antients' grand secretary, whom he terms 'the most remarkable mason of that time'. And he was correspondingly critical of the original Grand Lodge of England, especially Lord Byron, the grand master, and the core leadership, commenting that it was principally their actions and inactions that allowed the Antients to gain traction in London and elsewhere.

Sadler's assessment of the Antients focuses more directly - and correctly - on the influence of the majority 'Irish faction' in the rival Antients Grand Lodge and its constituent lodges. However, unlike Gould, Sadler argues pedantically that since the London Irish had not been members of English lodges it would be wrong to term any rivalry between the two organisations and their members a 'schism'.

Sadler's argument is based on a seeming tautology - that by definition one cannot leave or fracture an organisation of which one has not been a member. He therefore contends that no schism occurred and the presence of two competing grand lodges was an anomaly. This is a nonsense, albeit that it was accepted without serious question both at the time and subsequently. Indeed, Dashwood, writing in support of Sadler, makes a similarly faux legalistic statement that the position could not have been otherwise since no 'exclusive territorial jurisdiction [for grand lodges] had [then] been formulated'.[24]

Sadler's approach and that of subsequent commentators ignores the evidence and the reality. There *was* a cross over in membership between Moderns and Antients, and *vice versa*. Why else would each grand lodge

---

[23] R.F. Gould, *History of Freemasonry* (London, 1882-7), vol. 2, chapter 4; and Henry Sadler, *Masonic Facts and Fictions* (London, 1887), chapters 3-5.

[24] J.R. Dashwood (ed.), *Early Records of the Grand Lodge of England According to the Old Institutions* (London: Quatuor Coronati Lodge, 1958), QCA, vol XI, p.v.

threaten to sanction members who joined their respective rival? The Moderns insisted that their members meet only under their jurisdiction or risk expulsion.[25] And the Antients took a parallel view:

> *if any lodge under the ancient constitution of England... shall have in their possessions any authority from the Grand Lodge of Moderns or in any manner assemble or meet under such authority, [they] shall be deemed unworthy of associating with the members of the Ancient Community and the warrant they hold under this Right Worshipful Grand Lodge shall be immediately cancelled.*[26]

Sadler also disregards those among the London Irish who were prevented or dissuaded from joining English lodges, something that had been the case since the mid-1730s. And he may have purposefully overlooked freemasons who were ejected from Moderns freemasonry and resurfaced as Antients. Indeed, with almost a quarter of lodges expelled by the original Grand Lodge of England during the decade to 1750, that exodus is likely to have contributed substantially to the speed with which Antients freemasonry developed.

Returning to George Payne's rejection of the Irish deputation in 1735, there is a further issue: the offer of 'a new constitution here', in other words, the grant of a new masonic warrant by the Grand Lodge of England. Payne was aware of the key difference between Irish and English masonic warrants: the degree of autonomy devolved to an individual Irish lodge.

Although Irish lodges were nominally under the jurisdiction of the Grand Lodge of Ireland, in practice they retained considerable independence. Irish warrants delegated extensive powers to each lodge, including a license to draw up its own regulations and a grant in perpetuity to the master and wardens of the right to constitute the lodge. Irish lodges were thus not tied to a single geographic location but to the location of the warrant itself. It gave rise to the convention (and practice) that a lodge could meet anywhere, whether in Ireland or overseas. It was also the principle that underpinned the later grant of peripatetic military lodge warrants by the Irish and Antients grand lodges.

---

[25] Grand Lodge of England *Minutes*, 24 July 1755.
[26] Antients Grand Lodge *Minutes*, 1 June 1774.

This would have been anathema to the Grand Lodge of England and to George Payne in particular. Payne had been instrumental in the construction of the regulations that set out the centralised federal framework that governed English freemasonry and with other grand officers had spent over a decade promoting and enforcing them. His statement implies that if the Irish were to meet as regular masons in London they should do so only if they accepted an English constitution and observed English masonic norms, which included a more restrictive warrant.

Consequently, given the absence of any written letter of introduction from Lord Kingston - and perhaps even if one had been forthcoming – Payne's recognition of a deputation based on an Irish warrant would have posed an unacceptable threat to English masonic conventions.

One additional factor cannot be overlooked. Anti-Irish bigotry was common in the eighteenth and nineteenth centuries, something ignored by Songhurst, Gould and Sadler as a probable cause of the Irish deputation's rejection. Perhaps it was difficult to table such an explanation given the relatively recent union of Antients and Moderns and the substantially more socially-inclusive freemasonry that had followed as a consequence. And of course Gould and Sadler were writing in the 1880s when issues of masonic unity - and their absence - were once again to the fore.

At that time, an argument over the precise phraseology of the oath to be taken in lodges had divided international freemasonry, splitting the United Grand Lodge of England, the Grand Lodges of Ireland and Scotland, and the principal lodges of the United States and the British Empire from the Grand Orient of France and European and Latin American freemasonry.

And to add a final consideration, Songhurst, writing in 1913, could not but have been sensitive to the delicate question of contemporary Irish-English relations given the controversies surrounding the matter of Irish Home Rule.

Regardless, having had their overture rejected, the reaction of the Irish delegation to Grand Lodge is unknown: bemused, annoyed or otherwise. However, the development of Irish freemasonry in London continued untrammelled and became part of the London Irish community. After all, the Grand Lodge of England had no sanction other than exclusion and this worked in favour of an expatriate version of Irish freemasonry, helping to create a parallel environment in which it thrived.

In such circumstances it was understandable that London Irish masonry accentuated the greater deemed antiquity, integrity and superiority of their ritual, including the newly-introduced Royal Arch ceremony. And it was equally understandable that they would develop and emphasise mutual support, an aspect of Antients freemasonry that had particular social and economic relevance to a community facing adversity on several fronts.

Given these parameters there was, perhaps, an element of inevitability to the eventual aggregation of London's Irish lodges and the formation of a rival grand lodge that could provide an alternative font of prestige, patronage and authority, and that would function as a counterweight to the Grand Lodge of England.

Over time as the organisation grew, Antients freemasonry expanded to embrace the aspirational middle and lower ranks in England, America and elsewhere. After all, social and economic aspiration was not limited to the London Irish. Consequently, the Antients Grand Lodge and Antients freemasonry became a focal point for those seeking a more inclusive form of masonic association alongside greater mutuality and spirituality.

Perhaps the most vital element driving the new grand lodge forward was Laurence Dermott (1720-1791), the Antients' grand secretary (1752-70) and later deputy grand master (1771-77 and 1783-87).

From its inception Dermott positioned Antients freemasonry as part of a notionally long and well-established tradition. And it was in this context that he identified the Antients Grand Lodge with York freemasonry and took to describing the older and rival Grand Lodge of England as 'Moderns'. The moniker was intentionally pejorative at a time when the age and history of an institution had implications for its legitimacy and public standing. It was a clever and effective ploy. Indeed, virtually the same tactic had been employed by the premier Grand Lodge of England itself some three decades earlier.

A major part of the 1723 Constitutions is James Anderson's faux or traditional history of freemasonry that dates its origins to 'Adam, our first parent, [who] had the liberal sciences, particularly geometry, written on his heart'. In this Anderson mirrors the mediaeval guilds where the centrepiece of each of the Old Charges is an allegorical and romantic history dating freemasonry origins in England to the tenth century King Athelstan (the *c*.1390 Regius manuscript) or the third century St Alban (the *c*.1420 Cooke manuscript), one of the earliest English Christian martyrs, or even more remotely to biblical times. By positioning freemasonry as an institution that could be traced back across the centuries, the narrative implies if not insists upon authenticity and an antiquarian status. Dermott's dismissive categorisation of the original Grand Lodge as 'Moderns' and the adoption of the emotive title of 'Antients' was designed to reinforce the argument that the latter had the greater claim to chronological legitimacy. And through repetition and excellent press management, Dermott largely succeeded.

A mid- or later eighteenth-century multi-degree Antients masonic apron featuring the Royal Arch

The Aspirational London Irish

How many of the émigré Irish living in eighteenth-century London regarded themselves as 'London Irish' is unknown, but the probability is that few would have used that particular expression. The term is valid nonetheless and includes not just those who were Irish-born and had made their home in the city but also subsequent generations who retained their Irish identity.

There were perhaps four groups who can be placed under the general umbrella of 'London Irish'. The first consisted of those in London temporarily, whether for pleasure, study or business, or who intended to travel on to destinations elsewhere, not least Britain's American colonies. Alongside them was a second category of wealthy Irish aristocrats and gentry spending 'the season' in London before returning to their Irish estates, a number of whom had seats in the House of Commons or House of Lords. A third group included family members, almost always younger sons, based in London to protect their family's Irish interests and generate business in Britain and overseas. And then there was the final group, the largest, perhaps 85-90% of the total. This ran along a broad spectrum from relatively affluent middling professionals through lower-middling artisans and others working in London's patchwork of service and manufacturing industries, to the working poor and the destitute. Many in the latter categories lived in predominantly-Irish 'rookeries' – slums - where there was the hope and belief that their fellow countrymen might offer some support, albeit modest, and an expectation that the strict Poor Laws that governed financial support from the local parish would be enforced less onerously.

There is no clear or definitive information as to how many Irish lived in London in the eighteenth century nor the percentage of London's population that they represented. We can access fairly reasonable estimates of the number of Irish physicians, apothecaries, lawyers etc., and Irish members of professional societies, however, this covers only a small minority of the relevant population.

To find a more dependable guide we need to turn to proxy indicators. But before we do so it is important to mention that eighteenth-century population statistics in London and elsewhere are only approximations. The first formal census was undertaken in 1801 and even then those documented as Irish included only those who were Irish-born and excluded second and later generations of Irish heritage.

Academic assessments of the number of London Irish in the mid-eighteenth century range from around 10,000 to over 60,000. At the upper level this would be equivalent to some 10% of London's population, which stood at around 650,000 in 1750. And it is the latter, higher number that is the more probable.

One validation comes from a survey of attendees at the Westminster General Dispensary between 1774-81, where around one in eleven of those recorded were Irish, equivalent to c.9% of London's population in an area of the capital that was not regarded as being especially 'Irish'.[27] Another indicator is the membership of Antients freemasonry in London, the principal social association for the aspirational London Irish.

Remarkably, the Antients' 1756 membership register lists just over 1,000 members of what was then a predominantly (c.60-70%), London Irish organisation. If we assume that in the late 1750s only a relatively small proportion of the London Irish, say 8-10%, in line with middling London society as a whole, had sufficient funds to pay the required subscription fees and charitable contributions, and that only 40-50% became members, the number of London Irish, men, women and children, would be 50-60,000, or 8-9% of London's population. However, this is no more than an anecdotal supposition.

Although there had been Irish enclaves in London from the late seventeenth century, St Giles in particular, the number of Irish settling permanently in London rose steadily in the 1730s and 1740s.

In the seventeenth century and early decades of the eighteenth, migration had been predominantly seasonal with men and women travelling across the Irish Sea to work on the harvest, especially the farms that ringed London. And although this continued, Britain's nascent industrialisation and the lure of London's growing wealth created a locus of perceived opportunity that resulted in migration leading to permanent settlement.

Higher migration from Ireland was also driven by the appalling weather conditions of 1739 (the year in which the Thames froze in central London), and the two years that followed. The consistently

---

[27] Dr Robert Bland, 'Some calculations… the proportion of natives to the rest of the inhabitants of London', letter read at the Royal Society 10 May 1781, *Philosophical Transactions*, vol. LXX.

freezing conditions decimated Ireland's grain and potato crops and led to widespread famine. The impact was compounded by inadequate relief measures as well as ongoing trade restrictions which raised the cost of food imports and restricted the exports that could pay for them, and by the War of the Austrian Succession which inflated food prices across Europe and exacerbated food shortages still further.

Historians have estimated that up to 400,000 may have starved within an Irish population of *c.*3 million, a higher proportion than in the potato famine of the 1840s when *c.*1 million of Ireland's then *c.*8 million population died. And although Europe's weather returned to more benign conditions in 1742, the legacy of deprivation and distress left an indelible mark and continued to power migration to America and Britain, 'the nearest place that wasn't Ireland'.

From the late 1730s to the mid-eighteenth century, a torrent of skilled and unskilled Irish migrants washed across Britain's towns and cities in search of work, especially London. London's linen and silk industries drew Irish weavers to Spitalfields; others, mainly day labourers, looked for work in the construction trades in house building and in the extension of London's docks, warehouses and other infrastructure.

Another contributing factor was the dismissal policies of the British army and navy. When militias and regiments were disbanded, such as in the late 1740s following the defeat of the 1745 Jacobite Rising and at the end of the Seven Years' War, or when ships were withdrawn from the fleet, the lower ranks, up to a third of which were often Irish, were discharged onto the streets.

There were jobs for some. London, the largest city in Europe and the centre of Britain's growing Empire, had pockets of wealth that created multiple opportunities for artists and musicians, artisans and skilled labourers, as well as sucking in domestic servants, porters and sedan chairmen. And as the wealth trickled down ever narrowing channels into the poorer parts of London, hawkers and the unskilled all took their chances to scrape a living. Some succeeded, but many slid temporarily or permanently into begging, vagrancy and often criminality, where punishments were severe if caught, tried and convicted.

London's Irish communities were distributed across the capital but the majority congregated in four large slums: the contiguous rookeries of St Giles and St Martin's, the former known as 'Little Dublin', for obvious reasons, or 'the Holy Land', referencing the religious faith of its many Irish residents, and the latter 'Porridge Island' for its numerous 'porridges' or 'cook shops', the eighteenth-century equivalent of fast-food outlets. The other two rookeries were in the warren of alleys beyond the Tower of London running east from the Minories through East Smithfield and along the Ratcliffe Highway down to the docks; and in the arc of streets north-east of the City of London from Clerkenwell through Moorfields to Spitalfields. Conditions in all were dire, marked by crowded lodging houses and cramped and insanitary tenements.

Many properties were held on short leases from absentee freeholders with lessees controlling a single or sometimes several buildings. These were frequently sub-leased, either floor-by-floor or room-by-room, and those sub-tenants might further sub-let a part of a floor or room to a family or to individuals.

There was a hierarchy within each building with the least costly rooms at the top and rear, and the more expensive at the front on the ground and first floors. The worst location was the basement cellar. Damp, foul and windowless, it offered the cheapest available accommodation, unless it had been converted into a workshop or laundry.

The largest rooms were generally sub-divided, with sleeping spaces separated by rag curtains or makeshift partitions. An individual house might thus hold fifty men, women and children, each with access to a space marginally larger than the width of a narrow bed. These could be leased monthly, weekly, or even daily, with the poorest paying less than 1*d* per night for a strip of floor without a bed or blanket.

Frequently discriminated against by English landlords, the London Irish were often catered for by their compatriots, with a slew of Irish-owned, Irish-run lodging houses and tenements operating across the capital. They were complemented by Irish-owned chophouses, alehouses, gin shops and brothels, and Irish networks for fencing stolen goods.

A minority of London Irish prospered, a function of determination, luck and expertise, becoming successful traders, artisans or shop keepers. Others were engaged in the professions as teachers or apothecaries, or took on work as lawyers, doctors and barber-surgeons, serving their own communities as well as a stratum of the capital's more affluent inhabitants.

The Antient membership records illustrate this matrix of occupations comprehensively. After allowing for the duplication of entries in the

Antients Grand Register, middling and skilled artisans comprise over a quarter of those members whose occupations are disclosed. However, the actual number is likely to have been far higher. Although some of those described as a 'tailor', 'weaver' or 'painter' etc. would have been self-employed, many, probably most, were small-scale business owners and employers rather than employees. In the eighteenth century, the description 'painter', for example, would cover anyone engaged in that trade, employee or employer. An example is James Hagarty, the past master of Lodge No. 4, a master painter who at one time employed Laurence Dermott.

For those that flourished, London's rookeries were not the hopeless sink estates of literature but a font of aspiration and entrepreneurialism. But this could give rise to potential problems with their peers.

Many of the capital's working men saw the London Irish as a threat to their already poor rates of pay. And they were justified. When workers downed tools in protest at the low wages offered for the rebuilding of St Leonard's church, Shoreditch, the strike was broken by Irish labourers willing to undercut local pay. It was the trigger for anti-Irish riots that required the militia to be called out. And this was not a rarity.

The Daily Journal, 2 August 1736

Between nine and ten o'Clock a Mob of several hundred Men was assembled at Rosemary Lane, Rag Fair, with Clubs and other Weapons; where six of the Ringleaders went through several Streets, and with a loud Voice cried out, 'Who is an Englishmen, and for the good of his Country, let him put out Lights in his Windows'.

This put the Inhabitants in the utmost Consternation; and nothing was heard in the Streets, but Down with the Irish, and the Cries of poor Women and Children of that Nation, who were turned out of their Lodgings, and exposed to the Mercy of the Populace, the Housekeepers being apprehensive of Danger to themselves if they harboured them.

About ten o'Clock the Mob began to break the Windows of the few Houses that had no Lights, forcing open some of them, and dividing among them the Liquors of such that were Publick Houses.

Then the Mob went to Well-Street and broke the Windows of the House of Mr Welden at the Bull and Butcher, a Cookshop, and forcing in, broke to pieces great part of the Household Goods, and did other Mischief.

Afterwards dividing themselves into three Bodies, some of them went to Mr Resby's, an Alehouse in Well-Street, broke the Windows to pieces, and did other Damages. Others did the like at the Queen's Head, a Cook Shop in Mill-yard, Rag-fair. The White-hart Alehouse in Church Lane, the Gentleman and Porter in White-lion Street, kept by Mr Allen, and several others kept by Persons reputed to be Irish, underwent similar Misfortune. But there was no House demolished, as reported in one of the Evening Papers.

On intimation of these Violences, Clifford William Phillips, Esq., one of His Majesty's Justices of the Peace, in conjunction with Justice Farmer of Well-close Square, procured a Party of Grenadiers from the Tower; and the said Mr Phillips accompanying the Commanding Officer, endeavoured to appease the Tumult; but were obliged to use rough Means for that Purpose, before they could disperse the Mob; several of whom were wounded, and particularly one Best, who is in Danger of his Life by a Wound on his Breast, and J. Watts and Thomas Lovelock were also wounded in their Arms etc., for the Populace greatly abused he Soldiers and threw Stones at them at the Beginning of the Fray so that they were obliged to use Force to defend themselves.

Nine of the Rioters were seized that Night, and secured in the Watch-house, where a Party of Guards was set over them. The Grenadiers in several small Bodies patrolled the streets all night and dispersed several of the Mob who were assembling at East Smithfield.

On Saturday Morning the soldiers were relieved by other Parties from the Tower, who patrolling the Streets, kept the Mob pretty quiet. The same Day about ten o'Clock in the Morning, the nine rioters were carried from the Watch-house to the Tower, where they were examined before the Commanding Officer and Justice Phillips, Justice Farmer, and four others. The examination lasted until four o'Clock, when four were discharged on good security, and five sent to Newgate guarded by Musqueteers. About six o'Clock in the evening, one J.C., a Drayman passing through Limon-street to Rosemary-lane, by the House of Mr Allen mentioned above, he was taken up as one of the Persons concerned in breaking his Windows and carried before Justice Phillips, who not thinking proper to accept the security of 200l. offered for him, after a long Examination, sent him to Newgate under a Strong Guard of Soldiers.

The Soldiers were relieved in the evening by others from the Tower, who kept those Parts very quiet. Orders were proclaimed the same Day thereabouts, and at Shoreditch, etc. injoining the Inhabitants to keep within Doors their Children, Servants, Apprentices, etc., at half an Hour after 11 o'Clock at their Peril.

> But it is observable, that in Spital-fields two Irish Weavers were forced to compound with the Populace, by throwing themselves upon their Knees, discharging their Irish Servants, and giving away some Money to drink. On Saturday Night last about 12 o'Clock a Party of Horse Grenadiers went to those Parts and dispersed several of the Populace that were gathering on Tower-hill, and other Places. They patrolled through the Street and Fields till Yesterday Morning, when they returned to Whitehall. Yesterday the Trained Bands of the Tower Hamlet were placed there, and relieved those on Spital-fields, Shoreditch.

Those working outside the City walls were free from the constraints of the City guilds, and this proved attractive. Spitalfields, formerly the pastures owned by the New Hospital of St Mary without Bishopsgate, better known as St Mary's Hospital or 'St Mary Spital', was home to thousands of Irish and Huguenot refugees. Many of the terraced houses had been constructed to combine workers' housing with workshops and showrooms, with weaving on the upper floors where the light was best, accommodation in the middle and a sales area at ground level.

Irish weavers began to arrive in Spitalfields in significant numbers from the 1730s as the decline in Ireland's domestic industry forced linen and silk workers to seek work elsewhere. The irony of the Irish seeking refuge in the capital city of the country that was in large part to blame for their poverty may not have been lost on them.

But the main areas in which the London Irish congregated were the parishes of St Giles and St Martin's, one of London's worst slums and described as 'abounding in poverty'.[28] Walford's description in *Old and New London* provides an evocative perspective as he looks back to the late eighteenth century:[29]

> On both sides of the way were rows of chandlers' shops, low public houses, cook-shops - or rather cellars - for the accommodation of the poorer Irish, who even then formed a colony here... It is true, although the place bore anything but a reputable name, some of its residents were honestly employed, even in the humblest walks of industry... there was, at least, a floating population of 1,000 persons who had no fixed residence, and who hired their beds for the

---

[28] John Mottley, *A history and survey of the cities of London and Westminster* (London, 1733-5), vol. 2, p.756.

[29] Edward Walford, *Old and New London* (London: Cassell, Petter & Galpin, 1878), vol. 4, pp.480-9.

night in houses fitted up for the purpose. Some of these houses had each fifty beds, if such a term can be applied to the wretched materials on which their occupants reposed; the usual price was sixpence for a whole bed, or fourpence for half a one; and behind some of the houses there were cribs littered with straw, where the wretched might sleep for threepence. In one of the houses seventeen persons have been found sleeping in the same room, and these consisting of men and their wives, single men, single women, and children. Several houses frequently belonged to one person, and more than one lodging housekeeper amassed a handsome fortune by the mendicants of St Giles's and Bloomsbury. The furniture of the houses was of the most wretched description, and no persons but those sunk in vice, or draining the cup of misery to its very dregs, could frequent them. In some of the lodging-houses breakfast was supplied to the lodgers, and such was the avarice of the keeper, that the very loaves were made of a diminutive size in order to increase his profits.

St Martin's, south of St Giles, was a maze of over-crowded tenements ringed by Long Acre, the Haymarket, Drury Lane, the Strand and Charing Cross. The foetid alleys, courts and narrow lanes were unsafe, with many properties severely rundown as leases neared expiration. Landlords had few incentives to repair and buildings were let cheaply to 'the lowest of wretches'.[30]

An observer in 1750 suggested that one in four houses in St Giles was a gin-shop, however, like St Martin's, St Giles was also home to small-scale manufacturing and other commercial activities. And although St Martin's parish officers complained of the excessive use of spirits that they judged would encourage disorder and crime, there is no evidence that this was any greater than elsewhere in London.

The proximity of taverns to tenements is understandable. None of London's working poor and few of its better-off lower-middling owned a property or had access to permanent regular housing. Many rented space weekly or monthly, and all bar the wealthy would have preferred the relative comfort of a public bar or tavern to the over-crowded conditions 'at home'. Consequently, life centred on the inn and alehouse and given that where one 'lived' (or slept), might change month-to-month or week-to-week, an appropriate 'permanent' address was often the local

---

[30] M. Dorothy George, *London Life in the Eighteenth Century* (London: Penguin, 1966), fns pp.331-47. (First published 1925.)

alehouse. This was especially relevant in the rookeries, and around half the members listed in the Antients' Grand Register living in the contiguous slums of Seven Dials, St Martin's and St Giles give their address as such.

Although the minutes and membership records of the Antients Grand Lodge remain extant, relatively few records of individual Antients lodges have survived. However, those that have include Lodge No.20 which met at the Hampshire Hog in Goswell Street. The membership register, like others, suggests that Antients freemasonry was characterised by shared occupations and locations, and that a combination of social and business inter-connections drove lodge companionship. It confirms that Antients masonry was from its earliest years an association of family, neighbours and co-workers, the majority living and labouring close to one another in relatively compact districts. It was a medium in which a mutual support society might be expected to take root - and it did.

The Members of Lodge No.20
The Hampshire Hog, Goswell Street, London

Date	Name	Role	Occupation	Address
09.07.1753	John McCormick	WM	Silversmith	Horse Shoe Alley, Moorfields
	Samuel Galbraith	SW	Watchmaker	Great Arthur Street
	James Bedford	JW	Victualler	Crown, St Paul's Churchyard
	Thomas Warren		Britches Maker	Catherine Wheel Alley, Whitechapel
	John Houghton		Silversmith	Mrs Bow's, Fleet Lane
	Noblet O'Keefe	Sec	Watchmaker	Great Arthur Street
	John Hosier		Back Maker	Brick Lane, Old Street
20.08.1753	John Finch		Silversmith	Horse Shoe Alley, Moorfields
	Thomas Jones		Silversmith	Barley Bow, Mile End Green
01.10.1753	John Scovill		Clockmaker	Horse Shoe Alley, Moorfields
	John Cleminson		Silversmith	Green Gun, Mile End Green

Date	Name	Trade	Address
15.10.1753	Fenwick Weddrinton	Watchmaker	Shorter Street, Wellclose Square
	James Newham	Shoemaker	Daggers Court, Moorfields
	Samuel Welbeck	Gold Chain Maker	Ham[p]shire Ct. Whitechapel
14.01.1754	William Healy	Peruke Maker	St John's Square
18.02.1754	John Summers	Jeweller	Blue Anchor Alley Bunhill Row
28.03.1754	John Hogan	Tailor	Blackfriars
01.04.1754	William Beckerton	Watchmaker	Mr Maud, St Martin's Lane
20.05.1754	Thomas Weir	Hatter	Mitchel Street, St Luke's Church
	William Fox	Mariner	Horse Shoe Alley, Moorfields
29.07.1754	Paul Blunt	Mariner	'Gone to sea'
	William Green	Victualler	White Lion, White Lion Street
16.09.1754	Samuel Hutchins	Not known	Not known
05.05.1755	Robert Barnett	Victualler	Red Cross, Minories
25.05.1755	William Corp	Shoemaker	Great Arthur Street
02.06.1755	Thomas Dowsett	Shagreen Maker	Warwick Lane
	John Forsaith	Brewer	Bell Lane, Spitalfields
19.01.1756	George Lankston	Glover	Great Arthur Street

Seven members formed the lodge on 9 July 1753 and a further thirteen joined in the first twelve months. Of these, just over half were relatively well-off artisans including five silversmiths, four watchmakers, a clockmaker, a jeweller, and a gold chain maker.

John McCormick, the master, a silversmith living at Horse Shoe Alley, Moorfields, on the outskirts of the City, was responsible for inviting his neighbours, John Finch and John Scovill, to join. The minutes of 20 August record that 'John Scholefield [was] reported by the Master and Senior Warden to be made a mason on our regular Lodge night next ensuing'.

Other incoming members linked through silversmithing include John Houghton, Thomas Jones and John Cleminson. The minutes of 3 September note that 'John Cleminson [was] reported by the Master, Bro

Stone[s] and Bro Lewis M[aster] No.4 to be made a mason on our regular Lodge night next ensuing'. Similarly, Samuel Galbraith, a watchmaker living in Great Arthur Street on the northern rim of the City at the Barbican, was an associate of Noblet O'Keefe, another watchmaker at the same address. The minutes of 23 December 1753, record that 'Bro Galbraith reported Mr William Healy [a peruke maker of St John's Square, Spitalfields] to be a member of this most honourable and antient lodge of free and accepted mason[s]'. And on 6 May 1754, a 'Bro Weir [was] reported to become a member of our Lodge by Bro Galbraith'.

Six new members joined in the lodge's second year when membership reached a plateau. Exclusions that year, most for non-payment, equalled the number of new entrants. Two new members, William Green and Robert Barnett, both victuallers, lived east of the City at nearby Minories and Goodman's Fields. It is unclear at whose invitation they were invited but at this time freemasonry was open and those wishing to join would simply have needed to ask a known member.

The principal fulcrums on which the lodge turned were John McCormick, the first master, and Samuel Galbraith, the senior warden, who in 1755 was elected the Antients' junior grand warden. Galbraith's influence is evident in the volume of visitors from lodge No.3 of which he had been master and in the number of proposals he made with respect to new members.

Galbraith also financed the lodge's initial establishment. If his influence had been central to maintaining the lodge's vitality, his subsequent absence would provide a reasonable explanation for the lodge's demise in the latter part of 1756 following his return to Ireland in March that year.

Lodge No.20 offers an example of characteristics found elsewhere in Antients freemasonry: a concentration of local addresses, in this instance around the north-eastern and eastern perimeter of the City of London; related occupations, here principally within the jewellery and watch making trades; and a sense of an association of friends and colleagues. Although their numbers were relatively small, the membership register records that most members attended the twice monthly meetings regularly and with only limited absences: McCormick was away on five occasions in 1754; Galbraith was absent only once ('sick'); and the majority of other non-attendees failed to attend on only a handful of occasions.

There were a few exceptions. John Finch moved to Lisbon in January 1754. That he paid his lodge fees may suggest that his London freemasonry was of some use to him in Portugal. John Scovill and John Cleminson ceased to attend after May 1754. Like Finch, Cleminson paid his lodge fees despite having 'gone to the country', however, Scovill was later excluded for non-payment. Six others were similarly excluded: three in September 1754 and three in May 1755, one of whom is recorded as having been unwell for the entire year.

In a paper transcribing the minutes and describing the lodge, Songhurst notes that the minute book had been prepared in the first instance by Laurence Dermott, who received 8*s* for its supply and for writing out the by-laws and preparing the minutes of the first two meetings. The implication is that the lodge was relatively affluent; further evidence is that the tyler was Richard Gough, the grand tyler.

The lodge's by-laws set out the fees and fines levied in relation to various events and infringements. Based on a retail price index deflator, the fee per meeting of 1*s* 2*d* would be equivalent to *c.*£12 (USD15) today, which would have excluded any compulsory charitable contribution; and the dining fee of half a crown, 2*s* 6*d*, would be *c.*£25 (USD33). The adjustment of price data for inflation is not exact and the figures would be considerably higher (by a multiple of 7-10) if based on average earnings. Nonetheless, even at the lower level, the inference is that each member's earnings would necessarily have had to be relatively high and that joining such a lodge was status-enhancing. There may also have been an implicit assumption that the benefits of joining - social and financial - had a tangible value. Conversely, the cost was the main reason members were excluded for non-payment.

Unlike London lodges under the jurisdiction of the Grand Lodge of England where meetings tended to be suspended during the summer, a function of members leaving for the country, lodge No.20 met bi-weekly throughout the year. And members paid fees on each occasion, plus dining charges and a compulsory charitable contribution. Nevertheless, although relatively affluent, the lodge was not wealthy. Indeed, McCormick, when master, reportedly complained at a meeting of the Antients Grand Lodge that he had 'no jewels to open the Lodge'. However, his grumbling is not borne out by the lodge accounts, the first item of which notes the donation of 10*s* 6*d* from Bro. Hosier to purchase such jewels.

Contradicting the London Irish's faux reputation for insobriety, by-law eleven spelt out the penalties payable for drunkenness. It indicates that the members of the lodge considered their activities to have significance beyond the social and that lodge meetings should command an appropriate level of solemnity. Where levied, fines were payable 'the third lodge night after they are due, otherwise the transgressor shall have no vote in the lodge and if not cleared on St John's day, [he] shall be excluded'. Indeed, the sanction for a third offence was considerable: 'exclusion without certificate or benefits and notification to the Grand Lodge'.

Masonic ritual was central to lodge proceedings. The lectures given by the officers, members and visitors were not the scientific or self-improving addresses that had been and remained a part of at least some Moderns' lodge meetings but rather recitals and explanations of masonic ceremonial. Lectures 'in the Craft', 'in the first branch' (the initiation ceremony), or 'in the second part' (passing to the degree of a fellowcraft), were given at virtually every meeting and not limited to those where members were actually initiated, passed or raised.

An obvious question is whether the Antients' focus on and championing of a more ornate form of masonic ritual was a factor in the popularity of Antients freemasonry in England, Ireland and elsewhere. The answer is 'probably'. For many members it would have provided a substitute for Catholic liturgy or the ceremonial of their church in Ireland. Indeed, it is reasonable to suppose that émigré Irishmen, in the main poorly educated and at a distance from home, would have welcomed a spiritual form of freemasonry.

However, notwithstanding any quasi-religious or spiritual benefits, it is realistic to believe that the main advantages of lodge membership were economic and social. Individual lodges and the Antients Grand Lodge served as proto friendly societies as well as providing a forum for social interaction.

Lodge membership also testified to a member's financial standing, validating that he was not only 'a good man and true' but also someone whose fees were up-to-date. A membership certificate was thus evidence of financial rectitude and reliability, and could led to improved trade and employment opportunities. This was the case both in the latter part of the eighteenth century and in the nineteenth. One example is that of harbour pilots in the Americas and in Britain's colonies who used masonic pennants as identifiers when competing for trade from incoming vessels.

Antients' masonic membership certificates were not issued as a matter of course on becoming a mason but only upon request and only if the member was in good standing. Because such certificates were *de facto* masonic passports that allowed the bearer to be recognised and accepted by lodges elsewhere, and provided access to ready-made support structures, they were considered to be – and were - a valuable asset. The minutes of 2 September 1754, for example, record a Bro. Blunt requesting a membership certificate 'as he is going to Jamaica'. Only after discussion was the paperwork granted, 'received honourably, as he has paid all his dues in our lodge'. And in advance of Thomas Dowsett joining on 25 May 1755, introduced by Galbraith, his masonic standing and 'being worthy' of membership was proved by 'his certificate from Lodge No.218, Ireland', a lodge attached to the 48th Regiment of Foot.

'The Red Dragon'
Eighteenth-century tavern sign

The Affluent London Irish

At or near the financial and social pinnacle of those Irish expatriates who had made their homes in London were merchants, traders and landowners. In the coffee houses and taverns of Westminster and the City, with and without their advisors and agents, they debated and decried the legislation and regulations that affected Ireland, often seeking to change them to their advantage, something that became increasingly essential following the straight-jacket of the Dependency of Ireland on Great Britain Act. Lawyers were instructed, bankers consulted, contacts deployed and monies expended to influence policy and politicians, and to obtain and retain government contracts.

The combination of London's professional and financial resources and the densely intertwined political, legal and financial connections in the capital were instrumental to achieving success and bypassing failure.

London was awash with rival interests and the Irish lobby - perhaps lobbies would be a more appropriate characterisation - was one of many that competed aggressively for influence. An on-the-ground presence was vital and it was typical for wealthy Irish families, both Protestant and Catholic, merchants and landowners, to have a member of the family, often a younger son, representing them and safeguarding their interests. Influence could also be acquired through professional lobbyists and by trading and dealing through well-positioned English counterparties with the relevant connections. However, a family member was considered the best possible option. In the eighteenth century, if a matter was of commercial significance or especially sensitive, negotiations were best conducted either in person or via a trusted intermediary, preferably a close relative.

Some Irish families and businesses chose to conduct business directly and there was a regular ebb and flow of visitors travelling to London for that purpose. Despite the time-consuming and occasionally dangerous passage across the Irish Sea, by the mid-eighteenth century a visit to London had become relatively commonplace. Moreover, for many it was not only the means to a commercial end but also an opportunity to enjoy the wide range of social connections and myriad entertainments of all descriptions in Europe's largest and most vibrant city.

This included freemasonry, which had become an integral part of eighteenth-century sociability, both commercial and personal, and the lodge that met at the Ship behind the Royal Exchange fulfilled that function, providing a discrete space for association at an august level.

The Ship behind the Royal Exchange, 1723 [31]

John Leigh Esq. (Master)

Mr Cloud Stuart (SW)	Mr Nathaniel Gould (JW)
Mr John Gascoyne	Mr John Hope
Mr Albert Nesbitt	Mr William Bently
Mr John Mason	Henry Cunningham Esq.
Mr Joseph Gascoyne	Mr Henry Hope
Mr John Bourne	Sir James Tobin
Mr Ralph Knox	Mr Bearc. Stonehewer
Richard Warburton Esq.	Robert Allen Esq.
Mr Peter Webb	William Spaight Esq.
William Worth Esq.	Mr Benjamin Lambert
Benjamin Dry Esq.	Abraham Sharigley Esq.
Gerard Bourne Esq.	Captain Patrick Trahee
Mr Jonas Morris	Captain Lionel Beecher
Mr Row Hill	Mr Richard Fitzgerald
William Moreton Esq.	Leon Hatfield Esq.
Mr Springett Penn	Paul Minchell Esq.
Mr Thomas Watts	Mr John Pringle
William Hoar Esq.	Tiss. [Sisson] Putland Esq.
Mr Robert Waller	Mr William Richardson

Among the Irish merchant community in England, a key focal point was the Royal Exchange, which occupied a site at the heart of the City of London. As elsewhere in the City, commerce was based largely on financial self-interest and somewhat free of the religious constraints that existed elsewhere. Indeed, although prejudice remained, money was seen as interdenominational:

---

[31] The list was compiled on 15 May 1723. John Lane's *Masonic Records* gives the warrant date as 5 May 1723. The latter was probably the date when the lodge was recognised by the Grand Lodge rather than the date of inception.

> *Take a view of the Royal Exchange in London, a place more venerable than many courts of justice, where the representatives of all nations meet for the benefit of mankind. There the Jew, the Mahometan and the Christian transact together, as though they all professed the same religion and give the name of infidel to none but bankrupts.*[32]

The master of the lodge in 1723 was probably John Leigh of Rosegarland, New Ross, Co. Wexford. Leigh would later become MP for New Ross in the Irish Parliament, sitting as the second member for that seat from 1727-58. His family were joint patrons of the constituency and John's son, Robert, inherited the seat in 1758.

New Ross was a strategically important port in the eighteenth century with extensive trading links to England, the continent and America. The manor of Rosegarland had been granted to Leigh's uncle, Robert, by Charles II following the restoration, alongside more than 3,300 acres in Co. Wexford and Co. Kildare. John inherited the estates in 1727 and in 1723 when the lodge membership returns were compiled he was probably in London representing the family's interests.

Cloud Stewart, the senior warden, was Cloudesley Stewart, a descendant of the Stewart family of Athenry, Co. Tyrone. The name references Sir Cloudesley Shovel (1650-1707), admiral-of-the-fleet, the navy's most senior officer, with whom the Stewart family were associated through marriage:

> *Andrew Stewart, commonly called Captain Andrew Stewart, who, with Lord Castle Stewart, to whom he was related, and his (Andrew's) brother James... went from Scotland to Ireland about the year 1627. On his marriage, he obtained from Lord Castle Stewart the greater part of the manor of Castle Stewart, but afterwards built and resided on another seat near Stewart's Town, Co. Tyrone.*[33]

Andrew Stewart had four sons. James, the third, was also a naval officer. *Debrett's* records that he married one of Shovel's daughters: 'James, an officer of the Royal Navy, married ---, daughter of Admiral Sir

---

[32] Voltaire, *Letters Concerning the English Nation* (London: C. Davies, 1733), p.44.
[33] John Debrett (ed.), *The Baronetage of England* (London: F.C. & J. Rivington, 1831), 3rd edn., p.1120.

Cloudesley Shovel, and died gallantly in battle'. The same information is repeated in White's *Notes & Queries*[34] and in contemporary press reports.

Nathaniel Gould (1697-1738), the junior warden, a merchant, had trading interests across the Baltic, continental Europe and Turkey, and later the West Indies. He also had extensive investments in Ireland and a family connection and commercial tie to Munster-based Walter Gould, an attorney at the Court of Exchequer and senior warden of the Grand Lodge of Munster.

Nathaniel Gould served as a director of the Bank of England from 1722-37 (with statutory intervals), and deputy governor from 1737 until his death. The family were leading merchants in the City and prominent non-conformists. Nathaniel's father, John, was chairman of the East India Company, and his uncle, also Nathaniel, preceded him as a director of the Bank of England and as deputy governor (1709). He was governor from 1711-13. All were partners in *Gould & Co.*, 'one of the largest suppliers of hemp, pitch and tar to the Navy', and particularly active in the profitable and oligopolistic tobacco trade with Russia.

Following his uncle and father's death in 1728, Nathaniel Gould and his older brother, John (*d*.1740), another director of the East India Company and MP for New Shoreham from 1729-34, took over the management of *Gould & Co*. They subsequently invited Albert Nesbitt, a member of the lodge and another successful Irish merchant trader, to join the partnership. The offer was spurred (and consolidated) by Nesbitt's marriage in 1729 to their sister, Elizabeth, and the partnership was renamed *Gould & Nesbitt*. It grew to become one of the capital's most profitable merchant houses.

Like his uncle, Nathaniel Gould also obtained a seat in Parliament, in his case as MP for Wareham in 1729. A by-election had followed the death of Joseph Gascoyne, the incumbent, that year. He was, not coincidentally another member of the Lodge. Gould lost the seat in 1734 and did not stand again.

Albert Nesbitt (*d*.1753), a younger son, had been despatched to London in 1717 to launch *Nesbitt & Co.* and represent his family's extensive business interests, including their estates at Brenter and Malmusoy in Co. Donegal.

---

[34] William White, *Notes & Queries* (Oxford: OUP, 1893), vol. 87, p.255. Cloudesley Stewart is described as 'probably a descendant of James Stewart, a naval officer killed in battle (third son of Captain Andrew Stewart)'.

Nesbitt was extremely able and quickly achieved success in the Baltic trade, gravitating to live in some splendour at Cattle's Court on College Hill. But despite his achievements in London

> the Nesbitts never abandoned their Irish circles. Indeed, Irish connections appear to have been vital for the house at all times it was active in trade. The need for access to Irish markets as well as political and social favours from Irish contacts in London were factors that kept the Nesbitt's 'Irish' and involved in ethnic networks.[35]

In establishing his own trading house and forming a successful alliance through *Gould & Nesbitt*, Nesbitt was doing what other Irish younger sons had done before. However, sending a son to London was not the exclusive preserve of the Irish. The same pattern was followed by planters and merchants from America and the Caribbean, and by others. The presence of so many expatriates created a web of interlinked and sometimes inter-dependent commercial and social networks that extended into politics, with temporary alliances formed to achieve common objectives.

Nesbitt was particularly astute in using his family's commercial contacts in Cork and Kinsale, a mid-size port to the south west of Cork, to facilitate naval provisioning and it is not a coincidence that Jonas Morris, a scion of one of the most prominent Cork merchant-trading families, was invited to join the lodge. Nesbitt also worked closely with Hoare & Arnold, the Dublin bankers, a firm with which William Hoar, another member, was probably linked.

Alongside his Irish connections, Nesbitt developed other contacts that facilitated the growth of his various trading businesses, including a slew of relationships with a broad range Jewish, Catholic and Protestant merchant houses.

The importance of government provisioning contracts to the Nesbitt family was a key factor behind their political support for Sir Robert Walpole and the Duke of Newcastle. Nesbitt became an MP in 1741, standing unopposed at a by-election at Huntingdon. The constituency was within the sphere of influence of Lord Sandwich who wrote to Henry

---

[35] Craig Bailey, 'The Nesbitts of London and their Networks', in David Dickinson et al, *Irish and Scottish Mercantile Networks in Europe and Overseas in the Seventeenth and Eighteenth Centuries* (Gent: Academica Press, 2006), pp.231-50. Quote from p.233.

Pelham, the prime minister, commenting 'as for Mr Nesbitt, my only objection to him is that I can't choose him for Huntingdon without hurting if not endangering, my interest in that borough'.[36]

Nesbitt had been elected for Huntingdon in opposition to Sandwich's own electoral interest in the borough. As a concession he subsequently stood down and was nominated for Mitchell, a pocket borough in Cornwall with 40 electors which he represented as a government supporter from 1747 until his death.

By the early 1750s Nesbitt's wealth had grown significantly. At his death in 1753, and in addition to property in London, Sussex and Ireland, Nesbitt left legacies of more than £20,000 and an £800 annual annuity to his wife, a sum equivalent to the annual salary of the Crown's most senior officials.

His business interests were passed to his nephew, Arnold (d.1779), a younger son of Thomas Nesbitt of Lismore, Co. Cavan. Arnold had been mentored by his uncle and was a fellow partner at *Gould & Nesbitt*. He succeeded to his uncle's parliamentary seat at Mitchell, which he held until 1754, afterwards sitting for Winchelsea and Cricklade, the former a pocket borough in the gift of the Treasury and the latter 'filled by ministerial supporters without a contest'.[37]

A letter written by Arnold to the Duke of Newcastle on 7 March 1761 opens a window on the machinations and costs involved:

> *When I had the honour of succeeding my uncle in the last Parliament, as I undertook the risk of a large expense for sitting two years, it was agreed I should be chosen into the present Parliament at the small expense of £500. Notwithstanding this agreement, Mr. Pelham insisted upon my standing at Winchelsea with Mr. Hunter, being the most likely person to defeat Mr. Belchier, from the little property I then had there. I did not choose this undertaking as it threatened a very large expense, but Mr. Pelham insisted upon it, and it was agreed my expense was not to exceed £1,000... We baffled Mr Belchier in all his schemes both in the corporation and at law, but my*

---

[36] 25 May 1747 (N.S.), Newcastle (Clumber) MSS. Quoted in *The History of Parliament*: http://www.historyofparliamentonline.org/volume/1715-1754/member/nesbitt-albert-1753.

[37] R. Sedgwick (ed.), *The History of Parliament: the House of Commons 1715-1754* (1970).

expense instead of being £1,000, amounted to above £3,000, besides a pretty considerable annual expense since… in the course of the seven years I have sat for Winchelsea. I have made several purchases both in and about the town, and those not very inconsiderable…

I dare believe your Grace thinks I have great obligations for the different contracts I am concerned in… but give me leave to say from the present prospect of the great disadvantages we have ever laboured under both at home and abroad in the carrying on of this business, things carry a different face.

The Nesbitts' naval and military contracts were vast and included the supply of rations to troops in North America and Quebec. Political support for the government in Parliament was a *sine qua non* for their retention, as was the financial backing they provided. The Nesbitts were substantial investors in a Dublin bank which underwrote government debt. Arnold Nesbitt subscribed additional capital of £20,000 in 1757, £350,000 in 1759 and £450,000 in 1762.[38]

In all, three inter-linked generations of the Nesbitt family traded from London. They included John Nesbitt (1745-1779), who in 1778 became a partner in the Dublin bank in which Arnold was an investor and a partner in *Gould & Nesbitt*. On Arnold's death, John inherited his Winchelsea and Huntingdonshire estates as well as plantations in the Caribbean. He sat as MP for Winchelsea from 1780-90, and thereafter for Gatton (1790-96), and Bodmin (1796-1802). All three constituencies were government pocket boroughs.

By the end of the eighteenth century the Nesbitt family's vast portfolio included slave-worked Caribbean sugar plantations and the rum trade; provisioning military and naval forces in North America, the Caribbean and Ireland; coal mines and an iron foundry; a wine importing business; and merchant banks in Dublin and London.

Richard Fitzgerald was a nephew of George Fitzgerald, scion of Catholic landed gentry in Co. Waterford who established a London merchant trading house that carried the family's name. Fitzgerald exported Irish linen to Britain, North America, the Caribbean and Europe, and imported sugar, wines and tobacco. His firm, *George Fitzgerald & Co.*, worked closely with *Nesbitt & Co.* and *Gould & Nesbitt*,

---

[38] L. Namier & J. Brooke (eds), *ibid, 1754-1790* (1964). The current money value would be *c.* £100 million (*c.*USD130 million).
Cf. www.nationalarchives.gov.uk/currency-converter.

creating an inter-locking business that extended from naval and military provisioning to the Caribbean sugar and rum trade. They also cooperated in Anglo-French and French-Caribbean commerce, and in insurance.

Although his uncle, brother and his family remained Catholics, Richard conformed in 1735 to protect the family's assets from any legal challenge on inheritance. This was a well-trodden path followed by many other affluent Irish Catholic families. Suggesting that nothing had changed in substance, Richard's wife was Catholic and he remained on excellent terms with his 'papist' family.

London-Irish merchants, including the Fitzgeralds and Nesbitts, commonly represented third-party clients in Europe, America and the Caribbean. The relationships gave their principal trading activities greater resilience, a function of diversification and insider knowledge of trade flows. Indeed, the number of international Irish merchant houses exceeded fifty by the 1760s, a figure which excludes those houses that traded solely on their own account or were engaged exclusively in Anglo-Irish trade.

It is notable and significant that London's Irish merchant community did not divide along sectarian lines but built close inter-denominational connections based on shared commercial objectives. Most firms were located in the same area of the City of London, with some 40 in and around Cateaton Street, between Cheapside and Gresham Street. The district had historically been dominated by the cloth trade and included many firms that traded Irish linen.

The 1745 Linen Bounty Act provided an additional fillip for London's Irish merchant houses. The mechanism for receiving the bounty, which was limited to linens that did not compete with those manufactured in England, necessitated intermediation: Irish linen exported from Britain 'shall only be entitled to the Bounty if the property of some person resident in Great Britain or America'.

Accurate market intelligence became ever more important as trade expanded internationally during the eighteenth century, and partners and family members were often deployed to one or more of the principal waypoints for transatlantic navigation: the Canaries, Cadiz, Lisbon and other major continental ports. From there they arranged transhipments, oversaw local trading operations and took responsibility for the re-provisioning of vessels. Precise and timely information was vital for trade, banking and insurance, and was an especial imperative for those houses that provided short-term working capital facilities or cleared and issued bills of exchange, activities that had become increasingly significant. It was for this reason that London's Irish merchants were an essential part of the success of their American, Caribbean and Irish counterparts and correspondents.

Other merchants in the lodge included Henry Hope; Benjamin Dry, a vintner; and Ralph Knox, who with Samuel Mercer was a partner in *Knox & Mercer*, which focused on the transatlantic trade. Knox was also a director of the London Assurance Company and Royal Exchange Assurance. Their boards included other lodge members and traders, among them George Fitzgerald, William Snell and John Bourne. Gerard Bourne, another lodge member, was probably his brother. They were either the younger sons of the Bourne family of Burren, Co. Cork, or of Cournallane, Co. Carlow.

Sir James Tobin was a Catholic from Co. Kilkenny. His obituary describes him as 'formerly a captain of a ship in the United East India Company's service; but on some disgust went to Germany and became there the chief projector of the Ostend East India Company, for which he obtained the honour of knighthood from his imperial majesty'. Highly successful in his chosen occupation, Tobin left an estate worth around £40,000.

Brearcliffe Stonehewer (1695-1752), was another eminent City figure with long-standing connections to Ireland in a business he inherited from his father, William, also a London merchant. Brearcliffe, a member of the Skinners Company, was similarly a director of Royal Exchange Assurance and London Assurance. He also sat on the Court of Governors of the City-run Bridewell Prison and Hospital, a charitable institution. Appointment to the Court was prestigious and carried the right to nominate apprentices. The Court's business, generally delegated to sub-committees, included determining the fate of prisoners and apprentices and overseeing the hospital's property portfolio and other assets.

John Gascoyne, a merchant and director of the Royal Africa Company, was another member of Bridewell's Court of Governors. His father, Benjamin, owned extensive estates in Ireland, albeit that the family lived principally at Chiswick to the west of London, close to Lord Burlington at Chiswick House and William Hogarth.

Joseph Gascoyne (d.1729) was John's brother. He held a government sinecure as well as land and property in Dublin, part of which was rented to the Crown. Joseph defeated the opposition Tory MP at Wareham in 1722 and held the seat as a government supporter until his death. He was succeeded by Nathaniel Gould 'without opposition'.

A third brother was Sir Crisp Gascoyne (1700-61), who in 1752 was elected Lord Mayor of London. In 1725 their sister, Susannah, married Thomas Watts (d.1742), a fellow lodge member and a key figure at Sun Life, one of the capital's fire insurance companies. He was secretary from 1723-34 and cashier between 1726-41. John Mason, a merchant and another member of the lodge, was a witness at their wedding.

Following his marriage to Susannah, Watts ensured that John Gascoyne obtained a position at Sun Fire; he subsequently succeeded Watts as Sun Life's secretary. Crisp Gascoyne, Susannah's youngest brother, also gained a position at Sun Fire (1749-61), as did Watts's sons, Thomas and Hugh. Such patronage and nepotism were commonplace. Watts was MP for Mitchell (1734-41) and thereafter Tregony (1741-42).

The interlocking business links between the members of the lodge are significant. The most obvious are via their respective partnerships but there were also directorships in common across various City companies and the Bridewell Hospital. Their cooperation and exercise of mutual support epitomises eighteenth-century society.

John Hope (d.1740), an Ulster-based merchant and linen draper, inherited a thriving business from his father which he developed further to become one of the wealthiest members of Ireland's Quaker community. He cultivated and benefited from extensive commercial ties to other Irish Quakers, especially in Dublin, and had a range of business correspondents from Bristol to Manchester to London. He would have been a regular visitor to the capital.

William Worth (1698-1725) of Rathfarnham, Co. Dublin, was the grandson of a Baron of the Irish Exchequer. Following the Williamite Wars, the family's fortunes were cemented by a highly valuable commission to manage the Irish estates of the Duke of Ormonde, the Lord Lieutenant.

William Spaight, later a barrister, had estates at Six-Mile Bridge, Co. Clare, where he sat as a magistrate. He was probably in London to study for the bar at one of the Inns of Court, a requirement for Irish barristers. The Irish made up a significant part of the transient legal community in London with several chambers known for their Irish links. However, London's legal world was not limited to Protestants. Catholics also had a presence. Although prohibited from practicing as a solicitor or barrister in Ireland, they were permitted to specialise in conveyancing and property, where a formal legal qualification was not a requirement.

Peter Webb, was probably the Irish jeweller and banker of that name. In the 1720s he was at the apex of his profession with a large and profitable Anglo-Irish customer base.

Henry Cunningham from Mount Charles, Co. Donegal, had commercial links to *Nesbitt & Gould, Greg, Cunningham & Company*, an Irish merchant house with offices in New York and Belfast, and *Conyngham & Nesbitt*, an Irish-American firm based in Philadelphia whose senior partner was a relative, Redmond Conyngham, also from Co. Donegal. Cunningham was related to Cloud Stewart. Andrew Stewart's second son, Hugh, had married Margaret Morris of Mountjoy Castle and their eldest son, also Hugh, had married the daughter of William Cunningham of Co. Donegal.

Richard Warburton (1674-1747), served as an Irish MP and as chair of the Irish Accounts Committee. As MP for Portarlington (1715-27) and Ballykanill (1727-47), Warburton was involved mainly with parliamentary legislation concerning the militia and trade. The family estate at Garryhinch, Queen's County, now Co. Laois, dated to the early seventeenth century and family members had sat in the Irish Parliament almost continuously since that time.

Jonas Morris (d.1734), was in London in 1723 to represent the family's interests. On his return home he was elected MP for Cork, sitting from 1730 until his death. The Morris family, Quakers, had lived in Cork for at least a century.[39] A Jonas Morris had been mayor in 1659 and his mayoral seal displays the mark of a ship between two towers.

A descendant, Theodore Morris, was mayor in 1699, and another, also Jonas, was High Sheriff for Co. Cork in 1769.[40] The family was exceptionally well-connected politically and socially, with their daughters marrying into prominent local families. The family's influence also extended to London where the Quaker community had considerable

---

[39] John Windele, *Historical and Descriptive Notices of the City of Cork* (Cork: Luke H. Bolster, 1839), p.100.

[40] John Fitzgerald, *The Cork Remembrancer* (Cork: J. Sullivan, 1783), pp.146, 186: *Protestant Mayors & Sheriffs of Cork*. There is anecdotal evidence that he was mayor of Cork in 1651 during the Cromwellian wars.

political influence, not least through engaging expensive professional lobbyists.

William Hoar, alternatively 'Hore' and 'Hoare', was MP for Taghmon in the Irish Parliament. The family were Cork-based merchants and bankers with interests that spanned shipping, victualling and brewing. They were not related to the English banking family of the same name.

The Hoare family held land in Cork, Kerry and Limerick, and had built trading alliances through beneficial marriages and commercial partnerships. They had forged particularly strong links with the Irish Quaker community, with Joseph Hoare (d.1729) marrying into the Rogers family, Cork merchants, and his son, Samuel, into a London Irish Quaker merchant house.

William Richardson (c.1690-1755), from Somerset, Coleraine, Derry, was MP for Augher in the Irish Commons from 1727-55, a position associated with his role as agent for The Honourable The Irish Society. The organisation had been created by Royal Charter at the beginning of the seventeenth century to oblige the City of London livery companies to co-finance Londonderry's plantations and expedite English colonisation; it also funded the initial construction of Londonderry and Coleraine. As its agent, Richardson represented the Society's governing board whose directors were nominated by the City livery companies. He would have been a regular visitor to London.

John Pringle (d.1741), hailed from Caledon, Co. Tyrone. Descended from Scottish immigrants, he lived at Lyme Park, a large estate near the Armagh border, where he was a justice of the peace and agent for Margaret Hamilton, who had inherited in 1713.

Captain Lionel Beecher later served in Colonel John Wynyard's Regiment of Marines, raised in November 1739. Philip Crossle notes that the family lived at Sherhin, Co. Cork, and that a number were freemen of the City.

Captain Patrick Trahee (or 'Trehee'), a merchant captain, was the son of James Trehee, captain and owner of the *Crocodile*. Patrick had taken over his father's vessel in around 1709:

March 10. Yesterday morning the Guildford, Captain Patrick Trehee, of 327 Tuns [sic] and 22 Guns, homeward bound from Jamaica, but last from Lisbon, was unfortunately cast away on the flats between the Downs and the River, but all the men saved. Her cargo... was valued at £25,000.⁴¹

The ship was recovered and Trehee continued to sail her on the Jamaica run and to the Netherlands. He appears regularly in the press in the early decades of the eighteenth century and later became a director of Royal Exchange Assurance.

'Tiss. Putland' is a misspelling or abbreviation of Sisson Putland, the son of Thomas Putland (d.1723), 'a late eminent Merchant of this City... of Paradise Row, Chelsea'. Sisson and his brother, also Thomas, later relocated to Dublin. Thomas remained there but Sisson returned, moving to Spring Gardens, 'a very large open Place, with good built Houses, well inhabited... with good Gardens'. He also owned an estate at Little Berkhamsted in Hertfordshire. The *Gentleman's Magazine* described him succinctly as 'very rich';⁴² the *London Evening Post* is more informative:

> *Yesterday Morning died, very much lamented, after a long illness, in Spring Gardens, Charing Cross, Sisson Putland, Esq... he has left the bulk of his estate, which is very considerable, to his brother George Putland, Esq., and a very handsome legacy with his coach and horses to Miss Lindar, and to his man, a hundred pounds.*⁴³

Alongside Nathaniel Gould and Albert Nesbitt, the wealthiest lodge member was probably Springett Penn (d.1731), a Quaker, the grandson of William Penn who founded Pennsylvania. He inherited vast land holdings in Pennsylvania, in England, principally at Warminghurst, West Sussex, and in Ireland, where the Shanagarry estate had been granted to his great-grandfather, Admiral Sir William Penn, by Charles II in exchange for the strategic town of Macroom and its castle, a gift from Cromwell.

Springett Penn was in London regularly in connection with the legal obligations he retained with respect to Pennsylvania.⁴⁴ With William Penn's second wife, Hannah, Springett had inherited the right to govern

---

⁴¹ *Post Man and the Historical Account*, 10-12 March 1709.
⁴² *The Gentleman's Magazine*, vol. 8, March 1738, p.165.
⁴³ *London Evening Post*, 21-23 March 1738.
⁴⁴ *British Journal*, 23 February 1723.

the colony under the auspices of the Crown and their consent was required in connection with its administration:

> *1 March. - Declaration by Mrs. Penn that the royal approbation of Patrick Gordon to be Deputy Governor of Pennsylvania and the Three Lower Counties upon Delaware River, shall not be construed to diminish the right claimed by the Crown to the said Three Lower Counties. Signed, Hannah Penn, Signed, Springett Penn in the presence of S. Clement and Will. Penn.*

> *11 March. Order of King in Council. - Approving of appointment of Major Patrick Gordon as Deputy Governor of Pennsylvania, provided… that Springett and Hannah Penn make the declaration proposed.*[45]

> *18 April. Order in Council, approving the draught of instructions relating to the Acts of Trade for Springett Penn, Esquire, and Hannah Penn, widow, to be by them given to Major Gordon, Deputy Governor of Pennsylvania..*[46]

Penn was twenty-one in 1723, four years below the stated minimum age to be accepted as a freemason, but exceptions were made for those with wealth and social standing and Springett Penn fitted that bill precisely. There was a broad overlap between Penn's commercial and masonic networks, something seen in Penn's grant of leases on his Shanagarry estate to Munster freemasons including Thomas Wallis, a Munster grand warden, who held eight leases from Penn; Edward Webber of Cork, who held nine; and John Longfield of Castlemary, who succeeded Penn as deputy grand master. Penn was also linked through business to Walter Gould, Richard Longfield and John Gamble, all masons and prominent Cork landowners and merchants. Arguably, such commercial relationships would have formed without any masonic link but that there was a connection points to the relative ubiquity of masonry among Ireland's elites.

Drawn to London, the wealthy and well-connected members of the Ship behind the Royal Exchange shared other commonalities. Freemasonry had emerged in the 1720s as a leading-edge organisation that championed Enlightenment ideas. Its Constitutions set out new

---

[45] Cecil Headlam (ed.), *Calendar of State Papers Colonial, America and West Indies*, vol. 35, pp.29-43.
[46] K.H. Ledward (ed.), *Journals of the Board of Trade and Plantations*, vol. 5, pp.270-7.

principles to which freemasons were expected to adhere, advocated meritocracy, religious tolerance, knowledge of science and the arts, and societal and personal self-improvement. Masonic practices included the election of Officers subject to democratic accountability, with one member wielding one vote within the lodge, majority rule and written by-laws and regulations. They were part of an ideology – principles – based on meritocracy, egalitarianism and aspiration, and part of a drive towards Enlightened self-interest.

Was the lodge at The Ship behind the Royal Exchange representative of upper-middling London Irish society? Probably, and in several ways. The composition of the lodge and the dealing among its members makes plain that religious tolerance, meritocracy and self-improvement were shared values. The merchant and landowning elites in Dublin, Cork and London - Protestant, Catholic and Quaker - had found a way to interact successfully and it is reasonable to presume that they traded and socialised with far more in common than has generally been supposed.

Antients Freemasonry in America

At the beginning of most American lodge meetings, the master of the lodge will instruct the senior warden to order the deacons 'to take the word' from each of those present before the lodge is opened in the third degree. This piece of the ritual, alongside other elements, is not English but Irish and Antients, and its roots are embedded in the second half of the eighteenth century.

Around 400-450,000 Irish migrated to North America in the eighteenth century. They included Anglicans, Catholics and Quakers, but most, more than three-quarters, were Ulster Presbyterians, that is, Scots-Irish, unlike the predominantly Catholic Southern Irish who migrated in the nineteenth and early twentieth centuries.

The Scots-Irish were the descendants of the Lowland Scots who had been encouraged to colonise the Plantation of Ulster from the early 1600s to the end of the seventeenth century. As Presbyterians they were subject to Ireland's penal laws which restricted full legal rights to Anglicans - members of the Church of Ireland. But despite what is often claimed, their mass migration from Ireland was not due solely or mainly to religious and political discrimination, nor was it a function of the famines that had racked the country, although all these factors played a role. The main drivers were the financial hardship caused by excessive land rents and the mercantilist trade legislation that constrained Ireland, together with the pull of better economic prospects elsewhere.

Although the number of eighteenth-century Irish migrants is relatively modest when compared to the more than four million who left for America in the nineteenth and twentieth centuries, it was nonetheless significant – some 10-12% of America's white settler population that in 1780 stood at around 2.2 million.

Irish migrants were not spread evenly across the thirteen colonies. Most gravitated towards specific regions, predominantly western Pennsylvania, the frontier lands of western Virginia, and the Carolina Piedmont, a fertile plateau lying between the Atlantic coastal plain and the Appalachians where the Scots-Irish comprised up to half, and sometimes more, of the local population.

Until the eighteenth century and aside from the Navigation Acts of 1663, few laws limited Ireland's foreign trade and domestic markets more onerously than those of England and few duties were in place that affected Ireland alone. As discussed, the passage of the Wool Act in 1699 and the anti-Irish trade and excise legislation that followed changed everything. Ireland's exports lost unrestricted access to world markets and the tariffs, duties and compulsory routing through British ports made Irish agricultural and manufactured exports uncompetitive. This was intentional, and it was effective.

The impact was particularly harsh on Ireland's Ulster Presbyterians, a mix of tenant farmers, tradesmen and artisans, with a scattering of landowners. Between 1720 and the end of the eighteenth century around half of Ulster's Scots-Irish community migrated. Some left for England but a far more formidable number travelled west across the Atlantic. Those with agricultural leases and businesses that had value sold up and used the proceeds to pay their fares to America and acquire land. Those who didn't travelled as indentured labourers and worked for up to five years to pay their debts. They sailed from Belfast, Dublin and Londonderry, as well as Ireland's many minor ports, and their destinations were Charleston, New York, Baltimore, Boston and Philadelphia, the first and most important port of call for the vast majority.

Pennsylvania was both a destination in itself and a distribution point for onward settlement elsewhere. Ireland's links to the province dated to

William Penn, the founder, who had extensive estates in Ireland. But the more effective drivers were the letters from friends and relatives carrying positive first-hand accounts of life in America, and the glowing advertising pamphlets commissioned by land speculators and shipping agents. There would be taxes and hardships, but the former were lower than those levied at home and the latter considered to be more manageable. And unlike Ireland, America had inexpensive land from which good profits could be earned, plentiful food grown, and relative political and religious freedom.

In the final decades of the eighteenth century the number of migrants leaving Ulster was so considerable that Ireland's linen industry was under threat of collapse and the exodus of agricultural tenants rendered a few Irish estates unviable. And although migration slowed during the war years of 1775-83, it accelerated hard afterwards, with more than 10,000 leaving in 1784 alone, a number that increased in the years that followed.

London also attracted Irish émigrés, some of whom used it as a staging post before leaving for America. Estimates vary but in the 1750s, as noted above, the number of Irish migrants in London was probably in the order of 50-60,000.

For the majority of Irish émigrés with limited education and narrow skills, life was tough and work irregular and poorly-paid. And even when waged labour became more common in the second half of the century, working conditions were frequently sweated, with many forced to seek parish funds and charity to supplement their income.

But despite these barriers a minority of London's Irish émigrés climbed the social and financial ladder. The number of Irish artisans and Irish businesses expanded, as did those entering the professions. Many prospered to break free from poverty and it was from this section of aspirational London Irish society that Antients freemasonry was born.

There is a reason that Irish migrants formed and joined Antients' lodges: they were largely excluded from English freemasonry. As discussed, the split had relatively little to do with ritual. Although there were differences, most obviously the Royal Arch, these were exaggerated by both sides to create 'clear blue water' and both forms of ritual had far more in common than was admitted. The real areas of conflict were quasi-religious and social. Quasi-religious because the Grand Lodge of England was considered, correctly or otherwise, to have semi-secularised freemasonry by moving away from its spiritual core. And social because a considerable number of English freemasons wished their lodges to remain comparatively exclusive and disparaged Irish incomers.

With relatively few exceptions, the English elites disdained Ireland. And Moderns English freemasonry followed suit. Expatriate Irish freemasons in London were not viewed positively and those who sought to join a London lodge may well have been refused. There was a general contempt for Ireland, which was pictured as a backwater, and an unease, founded mainly in the caricature of the Irish as 'feckless', that they posed a severe threat to freemasonry's charitable funds.

The position was made clear at the top of the organisation with the Moderns' grand secretary, Samuel Spencer, reportedly telling an Irish applicant that 'your being an Antient Mason, you are not entitled to any of our charity. The ancient masons have a lodge at the Five Bells in the Strand and their secretary's name is Dermott. Our society is neither arch, royal arch or ancient so that you have no right to partake of our charity'.[47]

Spencer expanded his diatribe against Antients freemasonry and Laurence Dermott in particular in a pamphlet, *A Defence of Freemasonry*.[48] His description of a 'three-hour lecture' by 'a red-hot Hibernian' is sarcastic, as is his account of the initiation of a sedan chairman who, too poor to settle his lodge fees in full, pays half in cash and half via an IOU. The pamphlet denigrates the Antients as a 'disgrace to society' with 'scarcely a coat or shirt to their backs' who are to be found in ale houses 'hooting and hollooing'.

Spencer's view of the London Irish and Antients freemasonry was a distortion. The Antients' membership registers and minutes demonstrate that its members shared a desire for social and economic betterment and a wish to be part of polite society. This would also be the case in America and elsewhere.

Of course, on both sides of the Atlantic Antients freemasonry was not for the poorest. Membership and dining fees and the obligatory charitable contributions were set at levels too onerous for most working men. But for those who could afford to join there were many reasons to remain.

The five Irish-led lodges that in 1751 founded the London-based Antients Grand Committee, later the Antients Grand Lodge,[49] were

---

[47] Henry Sadler, *Masonic Facts and Fictions* (1887); Kessinger Publishing (2003).

[48] Anon., *A Defence of Free-Masonry as Practiced in the Regular Lodges, both Foreign and Domestic under the Constitution of the English Grand Master* (London, 1765).

[49] The Antients Grand Lodge was formed following a meeting at the Turk's Head

joined by another four lodges within twelve months and a further thirty within five years, by which point the number of members recorded in the central registers exceeded a thousand.[50] Within a further two decades the Antients had authority over 200 lodges across London, provincial England and overseas, a figure that excludes lodges chartered by the Provincial Grand Lodge of Pennsylvania and other overseas provincial grand lodges, and the many independent Antients lodges that operated without a warrant, especially in America.

Membership growth was underpinned in part by the decision of a former grand master of the Grand Lodge of Ireland, the Earl of Blessington, to accept the titular position of the Antients' grand master. And it was spurred by *Ahiman Rezon*, the Antients' book of constitutions.

Ahiman Rezon allowed Dermot to position the Antients as an organisation that would 'keep the ancient landmarks in view', terming the Grand Lodge of England 'Moderns' to enhance the Antients' status and raise doubts as to the Moderns' legitimacy. The book was immensely popular with six editions published in England during Dermott's lifetime and at least another six in the two decades to 1813. Over the same period more than twenty editions were printed in Ireland, while in North America it circulated widely and following Independence would provide the basis for the constitutions of most state grand lodges.

A minority of Irish and Scottish migrants were already freemasons when they arrived in America. Others were initiated afterwards. And as they moved to settle the back-country of Pennsylvania and Virginia and travelled south and west along the wagon trails to the Piedmont they carried their freemasonry with them. Indeed, the chartering of Antients and Irish lodges is well-documented from the mid-1750s.

Although many warrants were sourced from across the Atlantic, Pennsylvania also took a leading role in launching Antients freemasonry across the middle and southern colonies, constituting lodges both at home and in other provinces.

---

tavern in Greek Street on 17 July 1751. The meeting was attended by around 80 members of five lodges: the Turk's Head; The Cripple, Little Britain; The Cannon, Water Lane, Fleet Street; The Plaisterers' Arms, Gray's Inn Lane; and The Globe, Bridges Street, Covent Garden. The grand lodge referred to itself as a 'grand committee' until 27 December 1753.

[50] *Registers of the Grand Lodge of the Antients, 1751-1813.*

Pennsylvania's first move to adopt Antients freemasonry was recorded at the meeting of Antients Lodge No.1, 'the Grand Master's lodge', in London on 5 September 1759 when a petition was presented and granted for a provincial grand lodge warrant 'for the brethren at Philadelphia'. The petitioners were members of Lodge No.4, a lodge that unusually for Pennsylvania comprised mainly artisans and seamen. The warrant marks the beginning of Antients freemasonry's formal path into North America.

As grand secretary, Laurence Dermott drew up a 'proper answer' and tasked Joseph Read of Antients Lodge No.2 with conveying the positive news and the provincial warrant to Philadelphia. Within a decade Pennsylvania's Antients freemasons would reign supreme and Moderns freemasonry all but disappear from the province.

Antients freemasonry in Pennsylvania was placed under the jurisdiction of William Ball (1729-1810), the Antients' first provincial grand master. He was born north of Philadelphia at Hope Manor on the Delaware River and owned Richmond Hall, a 676-acre estate that his father, a Quaker merchant, had acquired in 1728.

Ball was a trader as well as a silversmith and goldsmith, a profession that often extended into banking. He had been initiated in Lodge No.2 (Pennsylvania Moderns) on 9 January 1751 and was passed and raised the same year.

As was customary, Ball agreed to be 're-made' an Antient in order to become provincial grand master-designate and this occurred on 10 January 1760 when he was entered, passed and raised; he was elected provincial grand master the following month.

A warrant confirming Ball's appointment was issued by London on 15 July 1761 but the ship carrying it was captured by the French. A replacement was issued which was also lost, with a second replacement finally arriving in Philadelphia in 1765.

However, notwithstanding the absence of a warrant from London, Ball was installed as provincial grand master on 2 February 1764. To accommodate the Antients growing popularity he split Lodge No.2 into two separate lodges, redesignated Lodge No.4 as Pennsylvania's Provincial Grand Lodge and over the next fifteen years warranted sixteen other lodges.

Lodges Warranted by William Ball, PGM
Pennsylvania (Antients)

Lodge	Location	Date
Lodge No.4	Philadelphia, PA	28.12.1772
Lodge No.5	Cantwell's Bridge, DE	24.06.1765
Lodge No.6	Georgetown, MD	23.05.1766
Lodge No.7	Chestertown, MD	not stated
Lodge No.8	Philadelphia, PA	24.06.1766
Lodge No.9	Lancaster, PA	-- -- 1766
Lodge No.10	Baskinridge, NJ	-- -- 1768
Lodge No.11	Newtown, PA	17.08.1768
Lodge No.12	Winchester, VA	04.10.1768
Lodge No.13	Philadelphia, PA	29.07.1769
Lodge No.14	Christiana Ferry, DE	27.12.1769
Lodge No.15	Fells Point, MD	28.01.1770
Lodge No.16	Baltimore, MD	21.09.1779
Lodge No.17	Chester Mills, MD	16.09.1773
Lodge No.18	Dover, DE	not stated
Lodge No.19	Pennsylvania Artillery Reg't	18.05.1779

Ball served continuously as provincial grand master from 1761-81 and following Independence was elected to serve again in 1795. He died in 1810 and was buried with full masonic honours.

Irish and Antients freemasonry was also carried to America by the British military, many of whose regiments were deployed to Ireland and granted travelling warrants by the Grand Lodge of Ireland prior to crossing the Atlantic. A smaller number of regiments received warrants directly from the Antients Grand Lodge in London, which was keen to encourage America's 'right worshipful and very worthy gentlemen' to join its version of the Craft.

But Irish migration was arguably the more powerful mid-eighteenth-century vector and across the Piedmont, and in North Carolina in particular, Antients and Irish lodges mark the path of Scots-Irish migration along America's wagon trails from the mid-eighteenth century onwards.

Caswell Brotherhood Lodge, for example, was located between the Upper Road and the Great Valley Road. Old Cone Lodge at Salisbury and

Phalanx Lodge at Charlotte were established on the lower reaches of the Great Wagon Trail. And Dornoch and Blandford-Bute lodges at Warrenton and Union Lodge at Fayetteville were located on the Fall Line Road.

Other North Carolina lodges mark Scots-Irish settlements on the western frontier east of the Blue Ridge Mountains: Chatham County Lodge, Independence Lodge, Pittsboro, and Rutherford Fellowship Lodge in Rutherford County.

Antients freemasonry flourished in America with a broad membership that united aspirational men across the frontier. Farmers and planters, artisans, store-keepers and tavern-owners, merchants and local office-holders and politicians, all became freemasons.

The Antients changed the demographics of American freemasonry which, although remaining relatively exclusive, had a far more open admissions policy than before, sourcing members from across a broader social spectrum than its Moderns counterpart.

The War of Independence cemented the dominance of the Antients over the Moderns in what was now the United States of America. Where from the 1730s until the early 1760s, America's elites had looked to England and to London in particular as the epitome of polite society, and had embraced English freemasonry as the embodiment of elite polite association, from the mid- and late 1760s other influences prevailed. In the pre-war years, Moderns freemasonry came to be associated with loyalism; in contrast, the Antients were linked with patriotism and revolution.

Post-Independence, Antients freemasonry developed as an integral part of the fabric of both rural and urban communities and restored some of the more spiritual aspects of masonic ritual. The gulf between America's remaining Moderns and its surging Antients also grew and in Pennsylvania reached an extreme such that when Benjamin Franklin, a former Moderns provincial grand master, returned from Europe in 1785 he was not permitted to enter a Pennsylvania lodge unless he agreed to be re-made an Antients freemason. He chose not to do so and his funeral in 1790 was neither marked nor attended by Philadelphia's freemasons.

But such hostility did not occur everywhere. In post-war North Carolina there was no apparent antagonism between Antients and Moderns and when letters were despatched in 1787 inviting the state's lodges to convene to establish a new state grand lodge and elect a grand master, all of North Carolina's lodges were invited and all agreed to submit to its jurisdiction.

Massachusetts, and Boston in particular, illuminates well the relative position of Antients and Moderns freemasonry before and after Independence. Before the war, Moderns freemasonry included within its ranks many of Boston's most important figures from the governor and members of the Council to the city's leading merchants, lawyers and shipowners. Being a freemason was an assertion of social standing and of one's gentility and philanthropy. The lodge – and there were many of them - was an effective and pleasant forum for networking and social interaction, with the provincial grand lodge acknowledging overtly that ultimate masonic authority lay with the Grand Lodge of England.

In contrast, Boston's Antients freemasons admitted those whose financial, political and social status were of a lesser distinction. Antients freemasonry was associated with Ireland and to a lesser extent Scotland, but mainly the insurgent 'Grand Lodge of England according to the Old Institutions' – the Antients - which had extended the democratization of freemasonry. Many of its leading figures were connected to the Sons of Liberty and republicanism and, importantly, the organisation enjoyed a high level of masonic autonomy.

By the time Independence had been achieved, Antients freemasonry was the fraternal association of choice for many at the forefront of the new political establishment. Its leaders embraced its inclusiveness, moral principles and Enlightenment philosophy, and they identified freemasonry with the common good, in particular the provision of charity and mutual assistance.

When John Rowe, the Moderns PGM for Massachusetts, died on 17 February 1787, his St John's Grand Lodge and Massachusetts' Moderns freemasonry had reached a nadir. The First and Second lodges of Boston had merged, the Third and Fourth ceased to exist, and many of Boston's Moderns had fled to Canada or England. For those who remained it is easy to appreciate why they would question the rationale of remaining subordinate to England, a country with which they had been at war. After several years of debate, the Antients voted in December 1791 to merge with the Moderns to create the Grand Lodge of Massachusetts. The rivals were united on 5 March 1792, with St John's the junior partner.

Meanwhile, back in Ireland

There are no references to the Grand Lodge of Ireland after 1725 and few that report on Irish freemasonry more broadly until March 1731, when the *Dublin Weekly Journal* published a report of a lodge meeting on 6 March held, once again, at the Yellow Lion in Warborough Street. The *Journal* notes that the Earl of Rosse, the grand master, the Hon. William Ponsonby, master, and his wardens, William Cooper and Rowly Hill, attended, and that among others present were 'Lord Kingston, the past grand master of the Grand Lodge of England; the Earl of Drogheda; Lord Southwell; John White; Abraham Creyton; Henry Plunket; Lawrence Toole; William Moseley; and Thomas Griffith, the grand secretary'. Those initiated at the meeting 'upon proper application' were the Rt Hon. Lord Tyrone, the Rt Hon. Lord Netterville, the Hon. Tho. Bligh, and the Hon. Henry Southwell, Esq., all 'in due form, admitted members of that Ancient and Right Worshipful Society'.

The politics of those present suggests, if not confirms, that Dublin freemasonry was pro-Hanoverian and definitively pro-establishment.

William Ponsonby was the first surviving son of Brabazon Ponsonby, later the 1st Earl of Bessborough, one of Ireland's more egregiously ambitious politicians. The family's political influence dated from the sixteenth century and the grant by Cromwell of extensive estates in Ireland in return for military service. Ponsonby represented Newtownards, Co. Down, from 1725-27, and thereafter Co. Kilkenny from 1728-58. In 1739 he married Lady Caroline Cavendish, the eldest daughter of the 3rd Duke of Devonshire, the Lord Lieutenant of Ireland. Ponsonby afterwards became his private secretary and advisor and was sworn a member of the Irish privy council.

Devonshire also gifted Ponsonby a seat in the British Parliament, where he was successively MP for Derby (1742-54), Saltash (1754-6) and Harwich (1756-8). His father-in-law's patronage also saw Ponsonby appointed a Lord of the Admiralty (1746-56), Lord of the Treasury (1756-9) and joint-Postmaster General (1759-62), the last a particularly remunerative sinecure. He was sworn to the British privy council in 1765.

With his elder son frequently in England, Brabazon re-invested his political ambitions in John, his younger son, who took over the seat at Newtownards in 1739 and two years later was appointed Secretary to the

Irish Revenue Commissioners under his father, the First Revenue Commissioner. Brabazon encouraged John to emulate his older brother and ally himself with the Devonshires. John did so, marrying Elizabeth Cavendish, Caroline's younger sister, in 1743. He succeeded his father as First Commissioner the following year and was positioned by the family to succeed Henry Boyle, the speaker of the Irish Commons, finally achieving that goal in 1756.

All three Ponsonbys, father and sons, were leading government supporters while it remained in their interests to remain so, and in the 1740s and 1750s were arguably the most powerful political family in Ireland and the main 'undertakers' who managed (or 'undertook'), parliamentary legislation on behalf of the British.

Also present at the Yellow Lion tavern was Edward Moore, the 5th Earl of Drogheda. He had inherited the title in 1727 and the same year married Sarah Ponsonby, William and John's sister. Their son, the 6th Earl, later Marquess of Drogheda, continued the family's pro-Hanoverian allegiance and in 1746 carried the British colours at Culloden. He also took after his father masonically, becoming grand master of the Grand Lodge of Ireland (1758-60).

Thomas Southwell, 2nd Baron Southwell, appointed to the Irish privy council in 1726, was governor of Co. Limerick. He was elected grand master of Ireland in 1743. Southwell was a Fellow of the Royal Society in London (1735), a member of the Dublin Society (1733-40), and a founder and first president of the Physico Historical Society, an antiquarian club formed in 1744 whose objectives included 'removing the prejudices under which Irish history laboured and of doing justice to the country'.

Southwell travelled to England in June 1731 on his appointment as Master of Horse to the Princess Royal on her marriage to the Prince of Orange and his wife's appointment as a Lady of the Bedchamber. The Grand Lodge of England minutes for 23 November 1732 note his presence, incorrectly describing him as 'Provincial Grand Master in Ireland'. Contemporary newspaper reports record him as the 'late Grand Master of Ireland' or 'late Provincial Grand Master of Ireland', but neither title is substantiated. However, if it were accurate, his (undocumented) election may have taken place after 1726 and prior to 1730 during the period that the Earl of Rosse was overseas.

On 7 June 1733 Southwell acted as proxy for the Earl of Strathmore at the latter's installation as grand master. The annual procession to the Grand Feast at the Mercers' Hall set off from Southwell's London town house in Little Grosvenor Street and it was Southwell, on Strathmore's behalf, who installed the incoming grand officers. Underlining what was then a formidable connection between Irish and English freemasonry, Southwell also presided at the next meeting of Grand Lodge on 13 December.

James King, 4th Baron Kingston, grand master of the Grand Lodge of England in 1729, was also in attendance at the Yellow Lion. Kingston became grand master of Ireland in 1731 and again in 1735, 1745 and 1746.

The baronetcy had been granted to Sir John King in 1660. He had commanded Boyle Castle at the time of the Irish uprising and fought against the 'rebel' army. He was subsequently sworn to the Irish privy council and appointed governor of Connaught and colonel of his own cavalry regiment. His loyalty and service were rewarded further with the grant of the Mitchelstown estate, around 100,000 acres across Cork, Limerick and Tipperary.

Although Robert King, the 2nd Baron, fought for William III, his younger brother, John, supported James II, following him into exile and converting to Catholicism. He was later outlawed. However, when John unexpectedly succeeded to the title following Robert's death, John sought a pardon. This was granted by the privy council in 1694. Despite parliamentary opposition, John recovered Mitchelstown from forfeit in 1708 and swore an oath of loyalty in 1715, taking his seat in the Irish House of Lords. The family's division of religious loyalty – Catholic and Protestant - had been manufactured to insure against the loss of the Mitchelstown estate and John's abjuration of Catholicism and conversion to Protestantism was entirely pragmatic.

James King, the 4th Baron, John's sole surviving son, had been born in France during his father's exile and petitioned for naturalisation as a child 'born out of her Majesty's allegiance, but [a] good Protestant' when his father returned to Mitchelstown. He inherited the estate and the baronetcy on his father's death and although he is sometimes referred to as a Jacobite sympathiser, there is no material evidence. The family's history is one of political realism, not idealism and ideology.

James King, Lord Kingston, was sworn an Irish privy councillor in 1729, the same year he became grand master of English Grand Lodge. His connections with freemasonry are well-documented. He was initiated at the Swan & Rummer on 8 June 1726: 'admitted into the Society of Free Masonry and made by [Desaguliers] the Deputy Grand Master'. The lodge had aristocratic links and among those present was William O'Brien, the 4th Earl of Inchiquin, grand master of England in 1727, a guest of Martin O'Connor, the master, who became junior grand warden the following year. Three others were initiated at the same time: Gerald de Courcy, the 24th Lord Kingsale, Ireland's most ancient baronetcy; Sir Winwood Moffat, a Scottish baronet; and Michael O'Bryan (O'Brien), an Irish lawyer at Gray's Inn.

Kingston's connections extended from Dublin to Munster, a county dominated by estates created through the wholesale confiscation of Catholic landholdings in the sixteenth century. He served as grand master of Munster in 1731, the same year that he was grand master of the Grand Lodge of Ireland.

A masonic lodge had existed in Cork since at least 27 December 1726, the earliest extant record of its proceedings. As in Dublin, Cork freemasonry was substantially Anglo-Irish. The master of the Munster lodge from 1726-28 was the Hon. James O'Brien, the younger brother of William, 4th Earl of Inchiquin, who sat as MP for Charleville from 1715-27 and for Youghal from 1727-60, both in Co. Cork. He also held the lucrative position of Collector of Customs at Drogheda, a reward for his pro-Hanoverian loyalty to Britain.

The Grand Lodge of Munster functioned principally as the chief lodge in the province. There are no records to show that it continued as such after 1731 and this was almost certainly at Kingston's behest as he sought to replicate England's centralised structure. His period as Munster's grand master brought the province into Dublin's nominal circle of influence and the following year it was the Grand Lodge of Ireland, not Munster, which granted a warrant to a new lodge in the province.

Munster (and Cork) had strong links to English freemasonry. James O'Brien may have been a member of the lodge at the Rummer, Charing Cross. And, as noted, Springett Penn, O'Brien's deputy, the grandson of William Penn, was a member of the Ship behind the Royal Exchange, as was Nathaniel Gould, a principal associate and relative of Walter Gould, Munster's senior grand warden.

Of the others present at the Yellow Lion, Sir Marcus Beresford represented Coleraine as MP until 1720 when he was raised to the Irish peerage as Viscount Tyrone. He took his seat the following year and in 1746 was created Earl of Tyrone. Beresford became grand master of Ireland in 1736, serving for two years. Lord Netterville was Nicholas Netterville, the 5th Viscount, grand master in 1732. The family was Anglo Catholic, tracing their origins to the Norman conquest. He was a nephew of the Earl of Rosse and sat in the Irish Parliament.

The Hon. Thomas Bligh was probably the son of Thomas Bligh of Rathmore, Co. Meath, and lieutenant colonel of Napier's Horse, later the 2nd Irish Horse. Bligh was appointed colonel of the 20th Foot in 1740 and served in Flanders in the War of Austrian Succession. He was promoted to brigadier general in 1745 and major general in 1747, when he was given the colonelcy of the 2nd Irish Horse. The last, the Hon. Henry Southwell, Thomas Southwell's younger brother, was MP for Limerick and deputy-governor of the county under his brother.

Lepper and Crossle argue that the absence of meetings of the Grand Lodge of Ireland between 1726 and 1730 was a function of Ireland's economic depression.[51] But since Irish Grand Lodge met during the even more dire famine of 1740-41, a more likely explanation is that the meetings were undocumented rather than non-existent. Rosse was away from Ireland from 1726 until mid-1729, and Griffith, the grand secretary, was seriously ill in 1727 and 1728. Nonetheless, the 1727 registration of Lodge No.2 in Dublin indicates that the Grand Lodge *was* functioning, at least administratively.

The 1730 publication of Pennell's Irish version of the 1723 Constitutions confirms that freemasonry continued to be popular. And on 10 April 1731, *Faulkner's Dublin Journal* reported a meeting of the 'masters and wardens of the lodges of freemasons in the City of Dublin, assembled at the Bull's Head in Fishamble Street'. The meeting had been called 'to consider some of the regulations for the good of that ancient and right Worshipful Society' and to elect Lord Kingston grand master for the ensuing year.[52] Kingston's installation on 7 July was reported in due course, as was the succession of Lord Netterville, his deputy, the following year:

---

[51] Lepper & Crossle, *History of the Grand Lodge of Ireland*, vol. I.
[52] *Faulkner's Dublin Journal*, 10 April 1731.

> last Tuesday being the 1st of August, a Grand Lodge of Free Masons was held at the Two Black Posts in Sycamore Alley. The Rt Hon the Lord Viscount Netterville being Grand Master, and the Rt Hon the Lord Viscount Kingsland Deputy Grand Master, James Brennan, M.D. and Robert Nugent, Esq.; were chosen Grand Wardens by the said Grand Lodge.[53]

Unusually among the Anglo-Irish elite that led the Grand Lodge of Ireland, Henry Benedict (1708-1774), 4th Viscount Barnewall of Kingsland, DGM in 1732 and grand master in 1733-4, was a member of a prominent Catholic family that had settled within the Pale. Like Netterville, Barnewall was related to the Earl of Rosse, his second cousin: his mother was the youngest daughter of Sir George Hamilton and Fanny Talbot, Countess of Tyrconnel.

Barnewall's father, like others within the Catholic gentry, had fought for James II and been outlawed. His estates were restored under the Treaty of Limerick, however, and although he swore an oath of allegiance Barnewall refused to take a second oath to repudiate the spiritual authority of the Pope. His son, who inherited in 1725, did the same. Both were denied a seat in the Irish House of Lords.

Barnewall was related to another Irish grand officer, Robert Nugent (1702-1788), of Carlanstown, Co. Westmeath, junior grand warden in 1732. As in England, the Grand Lodge of Ireland included those who identified with the patriotic opposition associated with Frederick, Prince of Wales, and Nugent was one of the more prominent figures in that camp.

Nugent had converted from Catholicism and was described as 'a jovial and voluptuous Irishman who had left popery for the Protestant religion, money and widows'. Nugent inherited a relatively modest income from his estates, worth around £1,500 per annum, but added to it greatly by marrying three wealthy widows. In particular, following the death of his first wife, he married the twice-widowed daughter of James Craggs, the Postmaster General, which brought him extensive assets and estates, including the pocket borough of St Mawes in Cornwall where Nugent sat as MP from 1741-54.

---

[53] *Daily Journal*, 12 August 1732.

The financial aspect of Nugent's three successive marriages achieved such notoriety that they were granted the honour of an adjective by Horace Walpole:

> *Lord Middlesex is going to be married to Miss Boyle, Lady Shannon's daughter; she has thirty thousand pounds, and may have as much more, if her mother, who is a plump widow, don't happen to Nugentize.*[54]

Nugent was an important creditor of the Prince of Wales and became comptroller of the prince's household in 1747. His loans were redeemed in kind by George III, with Nugent elevated to the Irish peerage as Viscount Clare (1757) and made an Earl (1776); he was also appointed a Lord of the Treasury (1754–9), privy councillor (1759), President of the Board of Trade (1766–8), and vice-treasurer of Ireland (1759-65, 1770-82).

Arthur Mohun St Leger, 3rd Viscount Doneraile (1718-1750), grand master in 1740 at the age of twenty-two, was another in the Prince of Wales's camp. St Leger was MP for Winchelsea from 1741-47 and a Gentleman of the Bedchamber to the prince. William O'Brien, 4th Earl of Inchiquin, was also a Gentleman of the Bedchamber, as was Edward Bligh, 2nd Earl of Darnley, grand master of the Grand Lodge of England in 1737, and Henry Brydges, Marquess of Carnarvon, grand master in 1738.

Whether supporters of George II or the Prince of Wales, throughout the 1730s and into the 1740s Hanoverian loyalists dominated the Grand Lodge of Ireland. They included Sir Marcus Beresford (1694-1763), grand master in 1736-37, who was MP for Coleraine from 1715-20. He was the son of Sir Tristram Beresford who had commanded a Protestant regiment in the Williamite Wars. Beresford's political constancy saw him elevated to the Irish peerage as Baron Beresford and Viscount Tyrone in 1720, and to Earl of Tyrone in 1746, a resurrection of his father-in-law's title.

Beresford was followed as grand master by Sir William Stewart, 3rd Viscount Mountjoy, who was created Earl of Blessington in 1745. Mentioned as a freemason in 1731 when a member of Viscount

---

[54] Horace Walpole (Lord Drover, ed.), *Letters of Horace Walpole, Earl of Orford, to Sir Horace Mann* (New York: George Dearborn, 1833), vol. I, p.299.

Montagu's Bear and Harrow lodge in Butcher Row near Temple Bar, London, Mountjoy was grand master of Ireland from 1738-40, but perhaps more significantly in a masonic context, as Earl of Blessington he gave his imprimatur to the Antients Grand Lodge in London, becoming the first noble grand master from 1756-60.

The Mountjoy family had settled in Ulster from Scotland in the sixteenth century and been loyal 'undertakers' in the Irish Parliament for six generations. Mountjoy's grandfather had fought against the Irish rebellion as commander of a regiment of foot and been created Viscount Mountjoy in 1682. He was suspected of disloyalty by Lord Tyrconnel, the Catholic commander of James II's army in Ireland, and sent on a false diplomatic mission to Paris where, as intended, he was arrested and imprisoned in the Bastille. Joining William III's army on his release in 1692, he was killed at Steenkerque later the same year. Mountjoy's father also took command of a foot regiment and advanced steadily to lieutenant general. In 1714, he was promoted Master General of the Ordnance, a cabinet post, given the colonelcy of a regiment of dragoons and made Keeper of the Great Seal.

Mountjoy became the 3rd Viscount in 1728, inheriting estates in Co. Tyrone and Co. Wicklow, plus property in England at Silchester and a town house in Mayfair. In 1748, consolidating his position as one of the great and good, Blessington was appointed governor of Co. Tyrone and sworn to the Irish privy council. He was reappointed in 1761 following the succession of George III and made governor of Carlisle Castle in 1763.

Blessington's political allegiance to the Hanoverians was absolute but it did not extend to its government. His forthright support for Irish agriculture and manufacturing and for free trade was so considerable that it was noted by London agents of the Caribbean interest in Parliament who sought his backing to reduce or abolish excise duties and other barriers.

Blessington firmly opposed the many constraints forced on Ireland, something expressed in his support for Antients freemasonry and in his membership of organisations ranging from the Incorporated Society for the Promotion of Protestant Working Schools in Ireland to the Dublin Society, where he was joined by other senior Irish freemasons.

Supported by the Irish Parliament, the Dublin Society was an expression of the belief that Ireland should be encouraged to reduce its dependency on England. More than a provincial counterpart to London's Royal Society or the French Royal Academy of Science, the Dublin Society attempted to improve national wealth through the practical application of science to agricultural and manufacturing. Experimentation, assessing alternative agricultural techniques and promoting best practice, placed it at the vanguard of scientific advancement not just in Ireland but internationally. The arts were also supported, with large prize funds or 'bounties' established to encourage Irish culture.

Support for the sciences and arts reflected the Society's position as an Irish champion offering a new and practical vision of the Irish nation. In 1733, just two years after its formation, the Dublin Society had 267 members, including sixteen peers and their sons; five members of the judiciary, including the lord chancellor; parliamentarians, including the speaker; as well as baronets, army officers, barristers, doctors, academics and 'men holding high positions in the world of commerce'. The Society obtained a royal charter in 1750 and in 1820 under the patronage of George IV was renamed the Royal Dublin Society.

British condescension towards the Irish and Ireland grated with Blessington. That John Perceval, 1st Earl of Egmont, and other Irish peers, were 'shouldered aside' in the procession marking the wedding of the Prince of Orange to George II's eldest daughter, and that Irish peers were unable to obtain recognition of their precedence captures the sense of alienation.[55] And this was mirrored masonically in Dublin's changing relationship with London. What had been a mutual fraternal association became antipathetic, something reflected in Blessington accepting the role of Antients grand master and, two years later, in the Grand Lodge of Ireland's recognition of the Antients Grand Lodge and the cessation of fraternal communications with the original Grand Lodge of England.

Blessington chose not to be reappointed grand master in 1760. He was replaced by Thomas Erskine, 6th Earl of Kellie [Kelly] (1732-1781), who was succeeded in turn in 1766 by the Hon. Thomas Mathew, one of the wealthiest and most influential commoners in Ireland. Mathew's estates purportedly generated an annual income that exceeded £30,000 and contemporaries believed that he had been promised a peerage, although ultimately it was his son who was ennobled.[56]

---

[55] Toby Barnard, *Improving Ireland?* (Dublin: Four Courts Press, 2008), p.123.
[56] Thomas Mathew's son, Francis, was created 1st Earl of Llandaff in 1797. Cf., St

Among Blessington's successors as grand masters of Ireland was the loyalist Charles Moore, 2nd Lord Tullamore (1712-1764); grand master from 1741-42, he served as an Irish privy councillor and the governor of King's County. He was created Earl Charleville in 1758 and took over as Muster Master General of Ireland the same year, following his father.

John Allen, 3rd Viscount Allen (1708-1745), sat as MP for Carysfoot from 1732-41 and for Co. Wicklow until 1742, when he succeeded and took his seat in the Irish House of Lords. He was grand master from 1744 until his death the following year from wounds sustained following an altercation with British troops stationed in Dublin:

His Lordship was at a house in Eustace Street. At twelve in the night, three dragoons making a noise in the street, he threw up the window and threatening them, adding as is not unusual with him a great deal of bad language. The dragoons returned it. He went out to them loaded with a pistol. At the first snapping of it, it did not fire. This irritated the dragoon who cut his fingers with his sword, upon which Lord Allen shot him.[57]

Lord Kingston returned on short notice to replace Allen and was followed in the chair by Sir Marmaduke Wyvill, 6th Baronet (1692-1754):

Wednesday last the 24th Inst. being the feast of St John the Baptist, the Grand Lodge of Free and Accepted Masons met according to ancient custom, with their usual ceremony, at their lodge room in Smock Alley, where Sir Marmaduke Wyvill, Bt., Postmaster General, was installed and proclaimed Grand Master of Masons in the Kingdom of Ireland for the ensuing year. The evening was concluded with ringing of bells, and the greatest demonstrations of joy that could be expressed on that occasion, among the true and worthy brethren of that antient and honourable fraternity.[58]

Wyvill was unique among Irish grand masters in that he was English. His main estate was at Constable Burton in Yorkshire and included a renowned stud farm. He was a firm Hanoverian loyalist, appointed clerk

---

James's Chronicle or the British Evening Post, 18-20 February 1762; *General Evening Post*, 8-11 November 1777; *Gazetteer and New Daily Advertiser*, 10 November 1777.
[57] *Faulkner's Dublin Journal*, 25 May 1745.
[58] *Faulkner's Dublin Journal*, 23 June 1747; *General Advertiser*, 6 July 1747.

to the Irish privy council in 1735 and serving as vice chamberlain to the queen. He was also well-connected within the British political establishment.

In 1716 he had married Carey Coke, the sister of Thomas Coke, later Lord Lovell and subsequently Earl of Leicester. Coke was Robert Walpole's neighbour in Norfolk and one of his staunchest parliamentary supporters. In addition to being made a peer, he was rewarded with the sinecure of joint-Postmaster General and, as such, was able to lever Wyvill into the position of Postmaster General for Ireland, a role he retained until his death. Coke also served as grand master of the Grand Lodge of England in 1731.

Robert King, Baron Kingsborough (1724-1755), to whom Edward Spratt dedicated his 1751 Irish Constitutions, was grand master from 1749-50. He sat as MP for Boyle from 1745-48, when he was elevated to the Irish House of Lords. King was succeeded as grand master by Lord George Sackville, the youngest son of the Duke of Dorset, then Lord Lieutenant of Ireland.

It was broadly from around this mid-point in the eighteenth century that the political tone within the Grand Lodge of Ireland began to change, becoming more nationalistic, later overtly so. The Hon. Thomas George Southwell (1721-1780), whose father had been grand master in 1743, was deputy grand master during Sackville's grand mastership and grand master in his own right from 1753-6. The family were loyalist Whigs but their burgeoning Irish nationalism is underlined by their opposition to the oppressive Declaratory Act and nationalist pro-Irish sympathies expressed in subsequent parliamentary debates. Brinsley Butler, Lord Newtown-Butler from 1756 and 2nd Earl Lanesborough from 1768, deputy grand master 1753-56 and grand master in 1757, took a similar political line and supported recognition of the Antients Grand Lodge, an act of masonic defiance that foreshadowed his later opposition to the government.

Despite the mounting financial pressure on Ireland, an effective political opposition took time to develop and resentment was initially 'kept within tolerable bounds'. The delay was a function of several factors, including a generational legacy of traditional Protestant Anglo-Irish loyalty to Britain and the strength and effectiveness of British patronage. Nonetheless, Britain's mercantilist policies slowly herded the once steadfast Anglo-Irish towards patriotic Irish nationalism. And as the eighteenth century progressed, irritation at Britain's condescension and the ever-growing opportunity cost of playing economic second fiddle began to be expressed in louder and more frequent demands for self-determination.

Irish economic subservience was a counterpoint to Britain's growing economic and financial success. And the cost of dependency, once accepted as necessary, had become too obvious and too onerous:

> *we are daily running in debt; our public funds prove deficient; our trade is diminished; our farmers are breaking condition; the value of land is lessened; money is scarce to a degree, and consequently our credit sinking.*

By the late 1750s the patriotic nationalist faction in the Irish Parliament could muster a majority. And in what was a period of economic and social Enlightenment, easing restrictions on trade had become both a moral and a financial imperative.

As Arthur Dobbs had commented two decades earlier, 'a flourishing trade gives encouragement to the industrious... increases the power of the nation; [and] puts it in the power of every prudent and industrious man in it to enjoy more of the innocent pleasures of life'.[59]

Different colonies would take their own routes to modify or escape Britain's mercantilist harness, ranging from the purchase of parliamentary seats by West Indian sugar planters to the Declaration of Independence by the American colonists. However, all were looking at similar goals: 'to promote the happiness of [their] nation... [and] to increase its power and wealth'.

At first the Irish argued that notwithstanding their need for military protection, their commercial interests were inseparable from rather than subservient to those of England. Indeed, Dobbs wrote that treating Ireland as a competitor to England was as unsophisticated as comparing 'the rest of England against London... as there are several trading towns in Britain very rich besides London... [and there is no reason] why Ireland might not have a share in the trade of the world, though never come into competition'.

---

[59] Arthur Dobbs, *An Essay on the Trade and Improvement of Ireland* (Dublin: J. Smith & W. Bruce, 1729), p.3.

Dobbs was naive. The intellectual origins of England's mercantilist policies lay in the financial analysis that Charles Davenant, an economist, had developed at the end of the seventeenth century. Building on Gregory King's *Observations*, [60] Davenant's fledgling theory of supply and demand and the positive impact of economic self-interest, allowed him to set out a theory of comparative advantage in international trade a century before that of David Ricardo. Davenant's insight was that trade was the key component of any nation's financial well-being and his theories were integrated into mainstream political thinking as successive governments chose to follow his rational and pragmatic approach. There was, however, a major problem: Ireland.

> *Ireland abounds in convenient ports, it is excellently situated for trade, capable of great improvements of all kinds, and able to nourish more than treble its present inhabitants... its soil, sward and turf are in a manner the same with ours, and proper to rear sheep, all [of] which... beget a reasonable fear that in time they may come to rival us in our most important manufacture.*[61]

Unsurprisingly, commercial and financial self-interest dictated London's political calculations. The planters of Ireland would be encouraged to prosper but only as far as was consistent 'with the welfare of England'. There were, however, risks to this approach, as Davenant noted:

> *if through a mistaken fear and jealousy of their future strength and greatness, we should either permit or contrive to let [Ireland] be dispeopled, poor, weak and dispirited, or if we should render them so uneasy as to incline the people to a desire for change... they must be prey to an invader.*[62]

Ireland's 'invader' would not be the physical assault of a foreign power but rather the inroads made by patriotic nationalism. Ireland's deteriorating relationship with Britain spurred the development of Irish nationalism. It was articulated in books, pamphlets and in the discussions of the Dublin Society whose members promoted national improvement

---

[60] Cf., Gregory King, *Natural and Political Observations and Conclusions upon the State and Condition of England* (London, 1696).
[61] Sir Charles Whitworth (ed.), Charles Davenant, *Political and Commercial Works*, vol. II (London, 1771), p.236.
[62] Ibid, p.237.

and the manufacture of goods in Ireland to offset the nation's economic dependency. Support for domestic products and objection to English goods became synonymous with Irish patriotism, particularly during periods of economic depression. Indeed, simply wearing Irish linen became a political statement in itself:

> *Ye noblemen in place or out,*
> *Ye Volunteers so brave and stout,*
> *Ye dames that flaunt at ball or rout,*
> *Wear Irish manufacture.*
>
> *Thus shall poor weavers get some pence,*
> *From hunger and from cold to fence*
> *Their wives and infants three months hence,*
> *By Irish manufacture.*[63]

Irish concerns percolated back to London through formal and informal channels but continued to be ignored. The antipathy in relations between the two countries grew and Clark is accurate in his argument that a lack of common political ground between the Irish and British establishments came at an excessively high cost.[64] Indeed, hostility to Dublin Castle and its parliamentary allies developed into a succession of constitutional quarrels that dominated Anglo Irish politics through the latter half of the eighteenth century and into the nineteenth.

As in America, this focused on the passage of money bills. Irish newspapers, pamphlets, open meetings and well-advertised dinners were used by the patriotic opposition from the Anglo-Irish elites to the more middling to demonstrate their hostility to London. And although the majority of anti-government articles and pamphlets were written anonymously (sedition still being a crime and Dublin Castle willing to levy fines and insist on imprisonment on conviction), dissent was widespread. Irish patriotism had entered the mainstream.

From the 1750s, the dispute with Britain and its Dublin placemen moved to the heart of Irish public debate. *Honesty the Best Policy or, the*

---

[63] 'Irish manufacture – A New Ballad', quoted in Henry Grattan, *Memoirs of the Life and Times of Henry Grattan* (London: Henry Colburn, 1839), vol. 2, p.136.

[64] J.C.D. Clark, 'Whig Tactics and Parliamentary Precedent: The English Management of Irish Politics, 1754-1756', *Historical Journal*, 21.2 (1978), 275-301.

History of Roger, satirising the clash between Henry Boyle, the speaker, and the Ponsonby family, rival oligarchs, ran to seven editions in 1752 with massive sales: 'I am well assured over five thousand copies are gone off'.

However, it is notable that Anglo-Irish hostility to Dublin Castle did not equate to anti-monarchism. Irish patriotism and Irish nationalism were fully compatible with and part of Irish loyalty to the Crown. Indeed, for the British government, one of the most worrying aspects of Irish patriotism was the espousal of loyalty to the king of Ireland and to Irish parliamentary rights as opposed to the exercise of power by Dublin Castle and the Church of Ireland on behalf of the British government.

The character and composition of the Anglo-Irish elites and its political and social connections with England had evolved and were at the heart of change. That the relationship between Dublin and London had deteriorated is axiomatic. It was a function of Britain's economic domination and the opportunity costs of restrictive trade legislation. The parliamentary dispute over the money bills was a symptom not a cause of discontent.

Britain may have seen its tax and policy impositions as purely administrative and not an exercise in political subjugation. But even if this had been objectively accurate, which is far from the case, Ireland's perspective differed. Dublin saw an intolerable straitjacket that imposed political and economic inferiority.

The 1750s money bills crisis was followed by opposition to Townshend's reform of the parliamentary 'undertaker' system that was so advantageous to London and the emergence of an overtly passionate patriotic opposition, the Irish Patriot Party, led by Henry Flood and then Henry Grattan. Both were freemasons, members of the First Volunteer Lodge, No.620 founded in 1783 by the Independent Dublin Volunteers.

Grattan and the Patriot Party argued for the abolition of trade restrictions on Irish exports and legislative independence for the Irish Parliament. They did not seek independence from Britain but rather parliamentary rule from Dublin, not London, under the Crown.

The revolution in trade in the eighteenth century had laid the foundations for Britain's industrialisation and social transformation. Inventions such as the Newcomen engine and hydraulic pumps multiplied productivity, driving down cost and prices and substituting primary production with manufacturing and services.

The contrast with Ireland was obvious, not least to Jonathan Swift:

I would be glad to know by what secret method it is that we grow a rich and flourishing people without liberty, trade, manufactures, inhabitants, money or the privilege of coining, without industry, labour or improvement of land, and with more than half the rents and profits of the whole kingdom annually exported for which we receive not a single farthing, and to make up all this, nothing worth mentioning except the linen of the north, a trade casual, corrupted, and at mercy, and some butter from Cork. If we do flourish, it must be against every law of nature and reason.[65]

Irish commerce did not improve, it foundered, a consequence of the 'narrow conception of national interests which... dominated English economic policy'. Ireland was strangled by legislation and made uncompetitive by excise duties. With limited domestic capital to invest and over-regulation and heavy restrictions on exports, Irish agriculture was unable to take up the economic slack or even provide for the domestic market and tariffs and excise duties made Irish manufactures overly expensive. Despite the endeavours of the Dublin Society and analogous organisations which attempted to improve Irish agriculture and cultivation, animal husbandry and manufactures, success on the scale that was necessary was impossible to achieve.

Ireland's core outputs – dairy products, grain and wool – all suffered. Where British agricultural production tripled between 1700 and 1800 and its industrial output accelerated from the mid-century, as did population growth, this did not occur in Ireland. And in the light of the failed harvests that caused dislocation and despair across the country it was ironic that the operations of the victualling yards that supplied the Navy and Britain's Caribbean colonies gave rise to the (false) conceit that Ireland as a whole produced a food surfeit – as Swift termed it, 'butter from Cork'.

Pitt the Younger's correspondence with the Duke of Rutland, as Lord Lieutenant of Ireland, contained insights that his predecessors lacked. And his statement of the need for a settlement or accommodation with Ireland that was reciprocal was both perceptive and accurate:

---

[65] Jonathan Swift, *A Short View of the State of Ireland* (Dublin, 1728).

> *In the relation of Great Britain with Ireland there can subsist but two possible principles of connection. The one, that which is exploded, of total subordination in Ireland, and of restrictions on her commerce for the benefit of this country, which was by this means enabled to bear the whole burden of the empire; the other is, what is now proposed to be confirmed and completed, that of an equal participation of all commercial advantages, and some proportion of the charge of protecting the general interest. If Ireland is at all connected with this country and to remain a member of the empire, she must make her option between these two principles, and she has wisely and justly made it for the latter... the great advantage that Ireland will derive is from the equal participation of our trade and of the benefits derived from our colonies.*[66]

Although Pitt was unwilling to relinquish any 'control on the executive government of the empire, which must reside here', he *was* willing to offer concessions, unlike previous administrations that had been less open to compromise. But what was offered in the 1780s was politically too little and far too late. Britain's subordination of Ireland had by now changed the political psychology of the Anglo-Irish and opened a gate to patriotic nationalism. Indeed, the underlying terms of Ireland's dependency had become capable of challenge, and was challenged.

Concerned that what had occurred across the Atlantic could be repeated in Ireland, Britain agreed trade dispensations and the constitution of 1782, which largely removed Poynings' Law and repealed the 1720 Declaratory Act. Britain also became far more circumspect in its use of parliamentary powers and repealed much restrictive legislation.[67] But such concessions would be short-lived.

Less than two decades later following the suppression of the Society of United Irishmen's 1798 rebellion, an amalgam of Catholics, Protestants and Dissenters, including many Irish freemasons, the 1800 Acts of Union forced the creation of the United Kingdom of Great Britain and Ireland and Ireland's Parliament ceased to exist. In the wake of this upheaval, all that followed was almost inevitable.

---

[66] Pitt to Rutland, 6 January 1785, in William Pitt, *Correspondence between William Pitt and Charles, Duke of Rutland, 1781-1787* (Edinburgh: W. Blackwood, 1890), pp.72-3.

[67] J.C. Beckett, 'Anglo-Irish Constitutional Relations in the Later Eighteenth Century' *Irish Historical Studies* 14.53 (1964), 20-38.

Laurence Dermott

It is not possible to explain the influence of Antient freemasonry without mentioning Laurence Dermott (1720-1791), who almost singlehandedly and virtually from inception shaped Antients freemasonry's persona and controlled its marketing and administration. Dermott led the Antients as grand secretary and then deputy grand master for over twenty-five years.[68] He dominated the organisation and his influence was unrivalled.

Dermott positioned Antients freemasonry as a traditional and well-established organisation: 'keeping the ancient landmarks in view'.[69] It was in this context that he identified the Antients Grand Lodge with York freemasonry and described the older and rival Grand Lodge of England as 'Moderns'. The description was and was intended to be pejorative at a time when the age and history of an institution had implications for its legitimacy and public standing. It was an astute move.

Dermott recognised the social value of history and tradition, and especially its emotional impact. And it was a mark of his confidence and intelligence that he was willing to satirise the concept of masonic historiography. In *Ahiman Rezon* Dermott writes in a note to his readers that he had determined to publish a history of freemasonry and had 'purchased all or most of the histories, constitutions, pocket companions and other pieces (on that subject) now extant in the English tongue'. However, having furnished himself with pens, ink and paper and surrounded himself with the relevant compositions, Dermott 'fell to dreaming' only to be woken a little later:

> *A young puppy that got into the room while I slept, and seizing my papers, ate a great part of them, and was then (between my legs) shaking and tearing the last sheet... Like one distracted (as in truth I was) I ran to the owner of the dog and demanded immediate satisfaction. He told me he would hang the cur, but at the same time he imagined I should be under more obligation to him for so doing than he was to me for what happened. In short, I looked upon it as a bad Omen and my late dread had made so great an impression on my mind that superstition got the better of me and called me to deviate from the general custom of my worthy predecessors otherwise I would have published a History of*

---

[68] Grand Secretary, 1752-70; Deputy Grand Master, 1771-77, 1783-87.
[69] Laurence Dermott, *Ahiman Rezon* (London, 1756), *Dedication*.

Masonry; and as this is rather an accident than a designed fault, I hope that the reader will look over it with a favourable eye.[70]

Dermott's irony and satire were deliberately at odds with the more ponderous style adopted by the Moderns' chroniclers: 'Doctor Anderson and Mr Spratt… Doctor D'Assigny and Doctor Desaguliers'. And his conversational introduction and relaxed style would come to epitomise the more open attitude adopted by the Antients and mark its greater accessibility and attraction to the middling and aspirational working class.

Dermot makes his appearance in the Antients' *General Register* on 1 February 1752 as one of two men proposed for the position of grand secretary to replace John Morgan, who had been 'lately appointed to an office on board one of His Majesty's ships'. His early life is subject to conjecture but the general consensus is that he was born on 24 June 1720 in Co. Roscommon and afterwards moved to Dublin.

Newspaper articles and advertisements confirm that the Dermott family were Dublin-based merchants who traded with the Baltic and continental Europe. The head of the family was Christopher Dermott (16..?-1721), who had premises at Usher's Quay in central Dublin. Christopher had one child, Thomas (1699-17.?), by his first wife or partner,[71] and five children by his second wife, a Catholic, one of whom, Anthony Dermott (1700-1784), would inherit the business. Thomas, Laurence's father, was also a merchant, trading mainly in Baltic timber and paper from New Row, the northern extension of Francis Street.

Laurence Dermott emigrated to England in 1747/48, working in London as a journeyman painter. In the Antients minutes of 13 July 1753 he writes that 'he was obliged to work twelve hours in the day for the Master Painter who employed him'. This was James Hagarty, a past master of lodge No.4 and chairman of the Grand Committee that approved Dermott as the new grand secretary.

In 1762 Dermott married Elizabeth Merryman, the widow of 'Mr Merryman, who kept the Wine Vaults in King Street, near Tower Hill'.[72] Elizabeth had been widowed in 1760 and her wedding to Dermott received appropriate press coverage:

---

[70] Ibid., pp.vi-xvi.
[71] They were possibly unmarried.
[72] *Lloyd's Evening Post and British Chronicle*, 13-15 August 1760.

> on Saturday last was married Mr Dermott, master of the Five Bells Tavern in the Strand, to Mrs Merryman, relict of the late Mr Merryman, an eminent wine merchant in Prince's Street, Tower Hill.[73]

The marriage was the second for her and the third for Dermott. A note in the *Public Ledger* a year earlier in November 1765 records Dermott's second marriage at St Clements Danes church to 'Mrs Mary Dwindle, Mistress of the Five Bells Tavern behind the New Church in the Strand'.[74] She was also a widow. The marriage lasted until Mary's unexpected death a short five months later.[75]

The Five Bells was a major enterprise and sufficiently large to accommodate concerts and public meetings. The tavern had a good reputation for hosting 'elegant entertainments' and formal dinners, as well as the usual drinking, dining and lodging rooms associated with such an establishment.[76]

Dermott would have been familiar with the Five Bells and its management. The Antients' Grand Committee met at the tavern regularly from December 1752 until 1771, when they transferred to the Half Moon in Cheapside. Indeed, Dermott was received his correspondence there: 'Mr Dermott, Secretary to the Grand Lodge of Free and Accepted Masons at the Five Bells in the Strand'.

Although he briefly managed the Five Bells as its landlord following Mary Dwindle's death, Dermott did not inherit the tavern. The freehold was held by the Worshipful Company of Haberdashers and the business was soon let to another publican.

Dermott had been initiated into lodge No.26 in Dublin in 1740 and rose through the various offices to become its Master in 1746:

> *Brother Dermott had faithfully served all Offices in a very reputable Lodge held in his house in the City of Dublin... [and] Brother Charles Byrne (Sr.), Master of No.2 proved that Bro. Lau. Dermott having faithfully served the Offices of Sr. and Jr. Deacon, Jr. and Sr. Wardens and Secretary was by him*

---

[73] *London Evening Post*, 15-18 November 1766; *Public Advertiser*, 19 November 1766.
[74] *Public Ledger*, 29 November 1765. His first wife, Susannah Neal, had died in 1764.
[75] *London Chronicle*, 27 February – 1 March 1766; *London Evening Post*, 27 February 1766.
[76] *London Daily Advertiser*, 9 April 1752; *Gazetteer & London Daily Advertiser*, 30 May 1763.

> Regularly Installed Master of the good lodge No.26 in the Kingdom of Ireland upon the 24th day of June 1746.[77]

The warrant under which the lodge was constituted had been issued in Co. Sligo in December 1735. The lodge then moved to Dublin where it met at Thomas Allen, the master's house, and from there to London, the warrant probably carried by either Allen or Dermott.[78]

The Antients' *General Register* lists Dermott's address in 1752 as Butler's Alley, Moorfields. It was close to Grub Street and immediately north of the City of London. Alexander Pope refers to the area in *The Dunciad* as a 'powerful image of shabbiness of way of life [and] morals'.[79] The area was impoverished, overcrowded and packed with cheap housing, brothels and gin and alehouses.

Following his marriage to Elizabeth Merryman, Dermott moved to King Street, St Botolph Aldgate, near the Tower of London, to manage his wife's vintner's business. Within a year of their marriage Elizabeth had a son. Named for his father, he was christened into the Church of England at St Botolph Without, Aldgate. He died aged 3 in 1770.

Alongside the money accrued from his marriages, Dermott also earned royalties from *Ahiman Rezon*, the Antients' book of constitutions. Dermott published *Ahiman Rezon, or Help to a Brother* in 1756 and, as mentioned, the book ran to at least six editions in England during his lifetime and another six or more afterwards. A further twenty editions were sold in Ireland. The text was based on Edward Spratt's Irish Constitutions, published in Dublin in 1751, itself based on the original 1723 Constitutions.[80]

Ahiman Rezon promoted Antients freemasonry successfully, arguing in favour of its greater antiquity and superior ritual as compared to the (not dissimilar) form practiced by the Moderns. Later editions highlighted the pact between the Antients and the grand lodges of Ireland and Scotland. The book's impact was considerable throughout England, Ireland and America, and grew as its message gained traction.

---

[77] Antients Grand Lodge *Minutes*, 1752-60, p.90.
[78] William Smith, *A Pocket Companion for Freemasons* (Dublin, 1735).
[79] Valerie Rumbold, *The Dunciad in Four Books* (Harlow; Pearson, 2009), p.4.
[80] A 2nd edn. was published in 1764; a 3rd in 1778; and later editions in 1779, 1780, 1782, 1795, 1797, 1800, 1801, 1807 and 1813.

The value of Dermott's royalties may have been considerable and in September 1785 in an act that set a seal on his standing within the Antients Grand Lodge, Dermott gifted them to the Antients' Grand Charity.

Notwithstanding his achievements and perhaps because of them, in the mid-nineteenth century, some four decades after the union and six decades after his death, it became commonplace to vilify Dermott. William Laurie wrote that:

> *much injury has been done to the cause of the Antients... by Laurence Dermott... the unfairness with which he has stated the proceedings of the Moderns, the bitterness with which he treats them and the quackery and vainglory with which he displays his superior knowledge, deserve to be reprobated by every class of Masons who are anxious for the purity of their Order and the preservation of the clarity and mildness which ought to characterise all their proceedings.*[81]

Albert Mackey described Dermott in a similar vein: 'as a polemic, he was sarcastic bitter, uncompromising and not altogether sincere or veracious'.[82] He nonetheless acknowledged that Dermott was 'in intellectual attainments... inferior to none... and in a philosophical appreciation of the character of the masonic institution he was in advance of the spirit of his age'.[83]

Robert Freke Gould's view of Dermott was of an 'unscrupulous writer [but] a matchless administrator'.[84] William Hughan called him 'absurd and ridiculous.[85] And Henry Sadler described Dermott's writings as 'comical', 'ridiculous' and 'scarcely worth a moment's thought'.[86]

Gould's observation that 'in masonic circles, Dermott was probably the best abused man of his time' was accurate. But the criticism was far from justified.

---

[81] William Alexander Laurie, *The History of Free Masonry and the Grand Lodge of Scotland* (Edinburgh: Seton & MacKenzie, 1859), fn. p.60.

[82] Albert Mackey, *An Encyclopaedia of Freemasonry* (Philadelphia, PA, 1874), p.214.

[83] Ibid.

[84] Dudley Wright (rev.), *Gould's Freemasonry Throughout the World* (New York, NY), vol. 2, p.151.

[85] William James Hughan, *Memorials of the Masonic Union* (Leicester, 1913), p.8.

[86] Henry Sadler, *Masonic Facts and Fictions* (London, 1887), pp.110-2.

Rolling with the punches, Dermott used subsequent editions of *Ahiman Rezon* to retaliate against his opponents with biting satire. He was effective, joking that the Moderns had found it

> *expedient to abolish the old custom of studying geometry in the lodge and some of the young brethren made it appear that a good knife and fork in the hands of a dextrous brother (over the right materials) would give greater satisfaction and add more to the rotundity of the lodge... from this improvement proceeded the laudable custom of charging to a public health to every third sentence that is spoke in the lodge.*[87]

And Dermott continued:

> *There was another old custom that gave umbrage to the young architects, i.e. the wearing of aprons, which made the gentlemen look like so many mechanics, therefore it was proposed, that no brother (for the future) should wear an apron. This proposal was rejected by the oldest members, who declared that the aprons were all the signs of masonry then remaining amongst them and for that reason they would keep and wear them. It was then proposed, that (as they were resolved to wear aprons) they should be turned upside down, in order to avoid appearing mechanical. This proposal took place and answered the design, for that which was formerly the lower part, was now fastened round the abdomen, and the bib and strings hung downwards, dangling in such manner as might convince the spectators that there was not a working mason amongst them. Agreeable as this alteration might seem to the gentlemen, nevertheless it was attended with an ugly circumstance: for, in traversing the lodge, the brethren were subject to tread upon the strings, which often caused them to fall with great violence, so that it was thought necessary to invent several methods of walking, in order to avoid treading upon the strings.*[88]

The Moderns published a rebuttal in 1765 in *A Defence of Freemasonry... as practiced in the regular lodges*, with advertisements for the book noting that it contained 'a refutation of Mr Dermott's ridiculous account of that ancient society, in... *Ahiman Rezon*'.[89]

---

[87] *Ahiman Rezon* (1764), pp xxix-xxxi.
[88] Ibid.
[89] *Gazetteer and New Daily Advertiser*, 21 September 1765.

This was an over-statement. *A Defence* achieved only the most limited success. Worse, the Earl of Blessington's acceptance of the position of grand master in 1756 and the subsequent decision of the Grand Lodge of Ireland to enter into communication with the Antients continued to dent the Moderns reputation (and was long-regarded by them with incredulity). Indeed, even a century later, Moderns apologists considered the decision inexplicable, Gould writing that it was 'a little singular that Dermott secured the services as titular grand master [of a] nobleman under whose presidency the Grand Lodge of Ireland conformed to the laws and regulations enacted by the Regular or Original Grand Lodge of England.'[90]

Gould was mistaken. He failed to appreciate the political and socio-economic dynamics that underlay Blessington's decision and why the Antients had enjoyed success in attracting members. In any event, even within the terms of his own analysis, Ireland had *adapted* rather than *adopted* the laws and regulations of the Grand Lodge of England.

Antients freemasonry expanded massively under Dermott's guidance. The combination of inclusivity and notionally superior antiquity was a powerful draw and in his second edition of *Ahiman Rezon*, Dermott composed a 'Philacteria for such gentleman as may be inclined to become Free-Masons' to accentuate the pre-eminence of Antients' ritual.

Probably more than any other element of *Ahiman Rezon*, the catechism captured and cemented the perception of masonic superiority, something that became key to attracting and retaining members.

Questions:

First: Whether freemasonry, as practiced in antients lodges, is   universal?
Answer: Yes

Second: Whether what is called modern masonry is universal?
Answer: No

Third: Whether there is any material difference between antient and modern?

---

[90] *Gould's Freemasonry Throughout the World*, vol. 2, p.168.

Answer:	A great deal, because an antient mason can not only make himself known to his brother but in cases of necessity can discover his very thoughts to him, in the presence of a modern, without being able to distinguish that either of them are free masons.
Fourth:	Whether a modern mason may with safety communicate all his secrets to an antient mason?
Answer:	Yes
Fifth:	Whether an antient mason may with the like safety communicate all his secrets to a modern mason without further ceremony?
Answer:	No. For as a Science comprehends an Art (though an artist cannot comprehend a science) even so antient masonry contains everything valuable amongst the modern, as well as many other things that cannot be revealed without additional ceremonies...
Ninth:	Whether the present members of modern lodges are blameable for deviating from the old landmarks?
Answer:	No. Because the innovation was made in the reign of George I and the new form was delivered as orthodox to the present members.
Tenth:	Therefore as it is natural for each party to maintain the orthodoxy of their Masonical preceptor, how shall we distinguish the original and most useful system?
Answer:	The number of antient masons compared with the moderns being as ninety-nine to one proves the universality of the old order...

Of course, what Dermott held out to be facts were either falsehoods or opinions. But they were nonetheless a powerful encouragement to join the Antients whether *ab initio* or by way of 're-making', that is, by converting from Moderns freemasonry.

The persuasive power of Dermott's arguments was directed at prospective candidates at home and overseas, and especially at American colonists whose 'right worshipful and very worthy gentlemen' were singled out for particular flattery.

As the Antients Grand Lodge expanded it posed a growing challenge to the authority of the original Grand Lodge of England. As an example, the frontispiece to the third edition of *Ahiman Rezon*, published in 1778, clearly reflects the exclusion and marginalisation of the Moderns in favour of the Irish, Scottish and Antients branches of freemasonry:

> *The three figures upon the dome represent the great masters of the tabernacle… The two crowned figures with that on their right hand represent the three great masters of the holy temple at Jerusalem. The three figures on the left hand represent the three great masters of the second temple at Jerusalem.*
>
> *The three columns bearing Masons aprons with the arms of England, Ireland and Scotland and supporting the whole fabric, represents the three Grand Masters… who wisely and nobly have formed a triple union to support the honour and dignity of the Ancient Craft, for which their Lordship's names will be honoured and revered while Freemasonry exists in these kingdoms.*[91]

Dermott's explanatory text reminded the reader that it was Antients freemasonry that offered the most support to the indigent, quoting an unfortunately phrased letter from the Moderns' grand secretary to 'a certified petitioner from Ireland' that stated that 'your being an Antient Mason, you are not entitled to any of our charity'. The letter continues, as noted above, confirming that Moderns freemasonry was not 'Arch, Royal Arch or Ancient [and] you have no right to… our charity'.

In short, the Moderns' response to the challenge posed by the Antients was to rule that no masonic charity would be available to any Antients freemason; that they would not be permitted to act as a tyler, a role often carried out by indigent freemasons; and that they would be excluded from all 'regular' lodge meetings.

Dermott heaped derision on the Moderns, underlining that Antients freemasonry provided a conduit for masonic benevolence, repeating the claim to superior ritual and suggesting that the Moderns Grand Lodge was both dictatorial and ignorant, asserting that they admitted 'all sorts of Masons without distinction', thereby confirming the Moderns' ignorance of the true nature of freemasonry 'as a blind man is in the art of mixing colour'.

Disparagement of the Moderns was a constant thread throughout Dermott's time in office, as was his vigilance in press management which ensured that the Antients would be portrayed positively:

---

[91] *Ahiman Rezon* (1778), 'Explanation of the Frontispiece'.

> the [3rd Duke of Atholl] thanked them for the great honour they had conferred upon him by continuing him Grand Master for the year ending and he likewise acquainted them that he was of opinion (and it is the opinion of the Society in general) the Modern Masons are acting entirely inconsistently with the antient customs and principles of the craft.[92]

The installation of the Earl of Antrim as grand master (and Dermott as his deputy) in December 1786 was a colossal occasion and was accompanied by the installation of officers of 'several hundred' Antients lodges. And Dermott once again ensured that the ceremony received widespread and favourable publicity. One press article, for example, reads that 'the day was spent in the utmost harmony and much to the honour of *the true system of ancient and legitimate masons*'.[93] It suggests that even after thirty-four years, Dermott was not willing to forego any opportunity to sideswipe the Moderns in order to place the Antients in a better light.[94]

Such antagonistic confrontation ended only after Dermott's death. The tone of later editions of *Ahiman Rezon* was moderated and the two grand lodges gradually eased towards one another as they attempted to close the ideological and social gap that separated them.

Discussions as to how to unite the Moderns and Antients began in earnest in the early 1800s. Reunion committees were formed in 1810 and thereafter things moved forward relatively swiftly.

It is important to note that the British royal family became involved in the rapprochement process and by so doing facilitated the combination of the two rival grand lodges at what was a time of significant political and societal unrest. Leaving aside the demeaning loss of the American colonies, the French Revolution in 1789 had been followed by war with France, a conflict that lasted until 1815 and Napoleon's defeat at Waterloo, and in the 1790s, Ireland had rebelled against British rule. Britain's establishment believed that insurrection was imminent and in 1799 passed the Unlawful Societies Act[95] and the following year pushed through the Acts of Union that abolished the Irish Parliament.

---

[92] *Middlesex Journal or Chronicle of Liberty*, 9-11 April 1772.
[93] My italics.
[94] *Morning Herald*, 29 December 1786.
[95] 39 Geo. 3. Preamble: 'a traitorous Conspiracy has long been carried on, in conjunction with the Persons from Time to Time exercising the Powers of Government in France, to

In the years prior to 1813, the Moderns' grand master was the Prince of Wales, later King George IV; he appointed the Earl of Moira and Prince Augustus Frederick, the Duke of Sussex, as his deputies. The Antients' grand master for much of the same period was the 4th Duke of Atholl who in 1812 stepped aside to make way for Prince Edward, the Duke of Kent.

The Duke of Sussex, Kent's brother, was installed as grand master of the Moderns in November 1813 and on the 25th of that month Articles of Union were signed by the two dukes at Kensington Palace. The Duke of Kent then stood down to leave the Duke of Sussex as grand master of the combined organisation – the United Grand Lodge of England.

The final hurdle had been to reach a compromise regarding the Royal Arch, which Dermott refers to in *Ahiman Rezon* as 'the root, heart and marrow of masonry'.[96] And in the context of any accord between the Modern and Antients this was potentially problematic.

The Royal Arch had become a hugely popular part of Antients ritual and had garnered a strong following. Indeed, members of Moderns lodges had also been attracted to the Royal Arch degree and the ritual had been embraced by the Moderns, albeit unofficially, from the 1760s.

However, despite what was happening on the ground, the Royal Arch degree had not been adopted formally by the original Grand Lodge of England. Indeed, it had been rejected, with Samuel Spencer, the grand secretary, announcing that the degree 'seduced the brethren' and did not and should not form part of the traditional ritual.

The Royal Arch had been for decades the most obvious means by which the two grand lodges were differentiated and its denunciation by the Moderns had provided Dermott with another highly effective means to malign them. The 1813 compromise was to define regular freemasonry to be 'the three degrees and no more... the Entered Apprentice, the Fellow Craft, and the Master Mason, including the Supreme Order of the Holy Royal Arch', the last being 'the master mason's degree completed'. That is the reason that the Royal Arch had such symbolic importance at the union of the Moderns and Antients, and it is why that legacy resonates today.

---

overturn the Laws, Constitution, and Government, and every existing Establishment, Civil and Ecclesiastical, both in Great Britain and Ireland , and to dissolve the Connection between the two Kingdoms, so necessary to the Security and Prosperity of both.'
[96] *Ahiman Rezon* (1756), p.47.

Ahiman Rezon, Frontispiece, 1764

The Antients' Early Lodges

The speed with which Antients lodges were established in London, across provincial Britain and internationally, was not less than remarkable. It suggests that many independent lodges were willing to accept the jurisdiction of a new grand lodge and demonstrates a vast latent demand. The latter should not be surprising. Moderns freemasonry had shown the way over the previous half-century, its Enlightenment message attracting a large aspirational following. Nonetheless, its relative exclusivity set a brake on potential future growth. In contrast and from the outset, Antients freemasonry attracted members from a far deeper and wider pool, and the expansion in membership and lodge numbers reflected this.

The first Antients lodges formed outside London were in Bristol (October 1753, lodges 24 & 25), where there were long-standing trading and masonic links with Ireland. Other Antients lodges followed, including Bridgend, Cardiff, Glasgow, Liverpool, Manchester, Plymouth, Coventry and Warrington. But growth was not exclusively in the ports and industrialising midlands and north. Canterbury, Exeter, Nottingham, Reading, Taunton and Worcester all hosted Antients lodges. And over the decades that followed the Antients built a broad presence across England from Kent to Cumbria and Devon to Durham, with many lodges formed in fast-growing urban communities where factory work and construction projects were plentiful, the canals in particular.

Antients freemasonry also expanded internationally. Lodges (often military), were formed in the Channel Islands, Gibraltar, Bermuda, Canada, the Caribbean and the West Indies, India, South Africa and elsewhere. Travelling warrants were issued to over sixty British regiments deployed across the Empire. And Antients freemasonry became established in the American colonies where lodges were warranted directly by London and indirectly by the Grand Lodge of Philadelphia. Indeed, some 600 Antients lodges were constituted in the second half of the eighteenth century.

Alongside them, lodges warranted by the Grand Lodge of Ireland worked in Australia and New Zealand; in North America, the West Indies and Latin America; and in India, Sri Lanka and China. And by 1813, Ireland had issued over 120 warrants to British army regiments.

The First Antients' Lodges

Lodge	Location	Year
No. 1	Grand Master's Lodge Initial meeting place not known but probably The Five Bells Tavern, Strand	1759
No.2	Turk's Head, Greek Street, Soho	1751
	Rising Sun, Suffolk Street, Haymarket	1752
	Thistle & Crown, Church Court, Strand	1752
	King's Head, Hewitt's Court, Strand	1754
No.3	Cripple, Little Britain	1751
	Crown, St Paul's Churchyard	1752
No.4	Cannon, Water Lane, Fleet Street	1751
	Temple & Sun, Shire Lane, Temple Bar	1752
	Red Hart, Shoe Lane, Covent Garden	1753
	Bedford Arms, Bedford Court, Covent Garden	1754
	Swan & Cross Keys, Long Acre	1755
No.5	Plaisterers' Arms, Little Gray's Inn Lane	1751
	Horse Shoe, Ludgate Hill	1752
	Red Lion, Dirty Lane, Long Acre	1754
No.6	Globe, Bridges Street, Covent Garden	1751
	Brown Bear, Strand	1752
	Rose & Crown, Clare Court, Drury Lane	1753
No.7	Fountain, Monmouth Street, Seven Dials	1752
No.8	Temple & Sun, Shire Lane, Temple Bar	1752
	Angel Inn, Wych Street, Strand (No.7 from 27 December 1752)	1754
No.9	Ship & Anchor, Quaker Street, Spitalfields	1752
	Admiral Vernon, Bishopsgate Street Without (No.8 from 27 December 1752)	1752
No.10	Duke's Head, Winfield Street, Spitalfields	1752
No.11	Thistle and Crown, Church Court, Strand (No.9 from 27 December 1752)	1752

No.12	Admiral Vernon, Bishopsgate Street Without (No.10 from 27 December 1752)	1768
No. 13	Carlisle Arms, Queen Street, Soho	1752
	White Hart, Shug Lane	1753
	White Swan, New Street, Covent Garden	1753
No.13	Mitre, Broadwall, Upper Ground, Southwark	1753
	Tiger's Head, Borough	1754
	Black Bull, Borough (No.11 from 27 December 1752)	1754
No.14	Carlisle Arms, Queen Street, Soho	1752
	White Hart, Shug Lane	1753
	White Swan, New Street, Covent Garden (No.12 from 27 December 1752)	1753
No.15	Marshalsea Tap House, Southwark	1753
	Tiger's Head, Borough	1753
	Black Bull, Borough (No.13 from 27 December 1752)	1754
No.16	Plaisterers' Arms, Little Grays Inn Lane	1752
	Thistle and Crown, Church Court, Strand	1753
	Turk's Head, East Street, Red Lion Square, Holborn	1754
	Crown, Crown Court, Fleet Street (No.14 from 27 December 1752)	1754
No.17	Scots Arms, Haymarket	1753
	White Hart, Shug Lane	1753
	Thirteen Cantons	1754
	Dorset Head, Villiers Street, York Buildings	1754
	Star and Garter, St Martin's Lane	1754
No.18	Admiral Vernon, Bishopsgate Street Without	1753
	Three Sugar Loaves, St John's Street	1754
	Bull & Butcher, Rag Fair	1754
No.19	Fountain Inn, Monmouth Street, Seven Dials	1753
	George, Broad Street, St Giles	1754
	Declared 'vacant, null and void' for non-payment	7 August 1754
No.20	The Hampshire Hog, Goswell Street	1753

No.21	One Tun, Strand	1753
No.21	Cheshire Cheese, Savoy Hill Alley	1754
No.22	King's Head, Little Suffolk Street	1753
	Bull's Head, St Martin's Lane	1754
No.23	White Lion, Hemmings Row	1753
	The George, Piccadilly	1754
	Prince of Wales's Head, Long Acre, Covent Garden	1754
No.24	Edinburgh Castle, Marsh Street, Bristol	1753
No.25	Unicorn, West Street, Lafford's Gate, Bristol	1753
	Three Indian Kings, Small Street, Bristol	1754
No.26	Rosemary Branch, Rosemary Lane	1753
No.27	Prince of Wales's Head, Capel Street, Rosemary Lane	1753
	Prince of Wales's Head, Rag Fair	1755
No.28	Royal Oak, Charing Cross	1753
No.29	The George, Piccadilly	1753
No.30	The Goat, Paved Alley, St James's Market	1754
	Scot's Arms, Haymarket	1755
No.31	Prince of Wales's Head, Butcher Row, Tower Hill	1754
No.32	Black Horse, Boswell Court, Carey Street	1754
	Woolpack, Long Acre	1755
No.34	Star and Garter, Panton Street, Haymarket	1754
No.35	King's Bench Prison, Southwark	1754
No.36	Blue Bell, Horse Alley, Moorfields, London	1754
	Red Cross, Minories, London	1754
	Red Lion, Jewin Street, Aldersgate Street, London	1755
No.37	King's Arms, Holywell Street, Strand	1755

Ahiman Rezon, Frontispiece, 1778

Military Lodges

The Grand Lodge of Ireland introduced the concept of travelling military warrants largely as a function of how lodge warrants were issued. Granted to the petitioning master and wardens and not tied to a tavern or other location, the lodge was able to meet at any place they chose. Moreover, lodges could operate not only in Ireland but also overseas. In contrast, in England, although lodges moved location from time-to-time, each warrant tended to be associated with a specific venue.

Although the Grand Lodge of Ireland sometimes issued travelling warrants to migrants and traders, many, perhaps most, were dispensed to British regiments posted to Ireland before deployment elsewhere. Because of this, military warrants became key to freemasonry's expansion across the British Empire. And although the Antients and (much later) the Moderns both followed suit, the Grand Lodge of Ireland led the way.

Military lodges were supposed to be closed to outsiders but in practice this was not the case and masonic membership 'leaked' into the local towns in which regiments were based. Community leaders would be invited to join the lodge as a member (with dispensation), or attend as a guest, and at least some petitioned to establish their own lodges once the regiment had moved on.

But although Ireland provided the catalyst for international expansion, the association of freemasonry with the military did not begin there. The 2nd Duke of Montagu, the first noble grand master of the Grand Lodge of England, held several prominent military positions. And these were not merely a function of his status as Marlborough's son-in-law. Montagu lobbied hard to be appointed to the 'right' roles, requesting the governorship of the Isle of Wight, for example, in order that he might 'be a military Man, that being a Military Post'.[97] Montagu also raised and financed his own regiments of Horse and Foot and was later captain and colonel of His Majesty's Own Troop of Horse Guards, later the 1st Life Guards, the army's premier cavalry regiment. He was also Master-General of the Ordnance, in command of the Royal Artillery and military supplies.

Montagu's importance in the military set an example to other senior officers, including Sir Adolphus Oughton and Sir Robert Rich, fellow

---

[97] *John Montagu, letter to Robert Walpole.* CUL: Chol. MSS 2008, *5 July 1734.*

members of the Duke of Richmond's Horn Tavern lodge. Oughton was colonel of the Coldstream Guards and the 8th Dragoon Guards. A pro-Hanoverian Whig, he was close to Frederick, Prince of Wales, indeed, his example may have been one of several factors in the latter's decision to become a freemason.

Robert Rich was a political fellow-traveller and also close to the Court, a Groom of the Bedchamber. He commanded successively the 13th Hussars, 8th Light Dragoons and the King's Regiment of Carabiniers where he succeeded his fellow freemason and member of the Horn, Lord Delorraine. Rich became commander-in-chief and Field Marshal in 1757.

Notwithstanding its extensive presence, there are few studies of freemasonry within Britain's military. Peter Clark in *British Clubs and Societies* comments briefly on the military aspects of freemasonry: 'for the middle ranks [on leave in London], a large array of military lodges appeared from the 1750s to keep tedium at bay'.[98] Clark also noted that 'many military lodges played a significant role in the colonies by admitting local civilians to the order'.[99]

Equally, few historians comment on how the endorsement of senior officers, some of whom were influential aristocrats, sanctioned and accelerated freemasonry's expansion within the army to the extent that it took on an important function at the core of regimental social activity and thus encouraged emulation. Examples include the lodge at the Sun Inn at Chester where Francis Columbine, the master of the lodge, commanded the 7th Foot. The lodge membership list for 1725 indicates that at least ten of the twenty-eight members were fellow officers including Colonel Herbert Laurence and Captain Hugh Warburton, the senior and junior wardens; Lieutenant-Colonel John Lee; Captains Charles Crosby, John Vanberg and Robert Frazier; Lieutenant William Tong; Ensign Charles Gordon; and the Cornet-of-Horse, Walter Warburton.

The Mitre at Reading was another military-connected lodge with at least a quarter of its members officers. Three were from the Horse Grenadier Guards: Major William Godolphin, Captain John Nangle, the adjutant, and Captain John Duvernett, senior Captain-of-Horse. Others included Captain Andrew Corner of the 7th Hussars and Captain John Knight. Similarly, a quarter of the members of the lodge at the Wool

---

[98] Peter Clark, *British Clubs and Societies 1580-1800* (New York: Oxford University Press, 2000), p. 127.
[99] *Ibid.*, p. 345.

Pack, Warwick, were military, including Colonel William Townsend, Captains William Tench, Robert Cornwall and Anthony Rankine, Lieutenant Thomas Dunning and Cornet William Chaworth.

Within the 3,000 or so members' names recorded by the Grand Lodge of England between 1723-35, the army was represented by over one hundred ranking officers. They included two who were later Field Marshals, twenty-three colonels, eight majors and fifty-six captains. But this tally excludes more than sixty dukes, earls, lords, barons and baronets who commanded their own regiments or otherwise held field rank.

Certain officers, not least Sir Jeffery (later Lord) Amherst, Britain's commander-in-chief in 1778, were particularly effective in facilitating military freemasonry. Amherst appears to have encouraged the formation of field lodges in the regiments under his command and of the nineteen he controlled in North America in 1758, thirteen had field lodges, ten warranted by the Grand Lodge of Ireland. With one exception, the remainder established lodges by the end of the decade.

Military lodges became part of regimental life: *the time passes very wearily, when the calendar does not furnish us with a loyal excuse for assembling in the evening we have recourse to a Freemasons Lodge,*[100] and for the local community: *we have about 30 or 40 Freemasons they have a fine Supper every Saturday night and often two or three in the week besides.*[101]

The expansion of freemasonry within the military, especially the army, had a political and diplomatic dimension that became more visible in the late eighteenth century and grew further as an instrument of Empire in the nineteenth. Alongside migration and trade, British military lodges carried freemasonry across the globe to North America and the Caribbean and to Asia, Australia and New Zealand. But it was the decision of the Grand Lodge of Ireland in 1732 to issue a warrant to the 1st Battalion, the Royal Scots, the 1st Foot, and to other regiments, that provided the initial impetus.

---

[100] John Knox (43rd Foot), *Journal of the Campaigns in America* (1769).
[101] The Egmont (Sir John Percival) Papers: Add. MSS. 46920-72130.

Military Warrants Issued by the Grand Lodge of Ireland

	Lodge Numbers & Warrant Dates
Cavalry Regiments	
2nd The Queen's Bays	960 (1805-34)
4th Royal Irish Dragoon Guards	295 (1757-96)
5th (Princess Charlotte of Wales) Dragoon Guards	277 (1757-1818) 570 (1863-)
6th Dragoon Guards, the Carabiniers	577 (1780-99) exchanged for 876, (1799-1858)
7th (Princess Royals) Dragoon Guards – the Black Horse	305 (1758) exchanged for 7, (1817-55)
1st or Blue Irish Horse, later 4th Dragoon Guards	295 (1758-)
2nd or Green Irish Horse, later 5th Dragoon Guards	277 (1757-1818) 570 (1780-1824) 44 reissued (1863-)
3rd or Irish Horse, later 6th Dragoon Guards	577 (1780) 876 issued 1799 in lieu of 577, lost 1794
4th or Black Irish Horse, later 7th Dragoon Guards	305 (1758) exchanged for 7, 1817
4th Dragoons – Queen's Own Hussars	50 (1815) exchanged for 4, 1818 & cancelled 1821
5th Dragoons – Queen's Own Hussars	289 (1757-96) 297 (1758-1818)
5th Royal Irish Lancers	595 (1914-1922)
8th Dragoons – Kings Royal Irish Hussars	280 (1757-1815) 646 (1932-80)
9th Dragoons – Queen's Royal Lancers	158 (1747-1815) 356 (1760-1818)
12th Dragoons – Royal Lancers (Prince of Wales)	179 (1804-17) exchanged for 12 (1817-27) 179 (1868-91) 255 (1755-1815)
13th Dragoons - Hussars	234 (1752-1815) 400 (1791-1849) 607 (1782-89)
14th Dragoons – King's Hussars	273 (1756-1827)

16th Dragoons – Queen's Lancers	929 (1803-21)
17th Dragoons – Lancers (Duke of Cambridge Own)	218 (1873-83)
	478 (1769-1801)
18th Lord Drogheda's Light Dragoons – 1 Squadron	388 (1762-1813)
18th Lord Drogheda's Light Dragoons – 2 Squadron	389 (1762-1821)
20th Jamaica Light Dragoons	759 (1792-1815)
23rd Light Dragoons (1794-1802)	873 (1799-1802)
23rd (26th) Light Dragoons (1802-1817)	164 (1808-17)

Artillery

7th Battalion, Royal Artillery	68 (1813-34)
	226 (1810-25)
9th Battalion, Royal Artillery	313 (1823-28)
Royal Irish Artillery	374 (1761-1818)
	528 (1781-87)
Corps of Artillery Drivers	241 (1811, not issued)

Regiments of the Line

1st Foot, Royal Scots 1st Battalion	11 (1732-1847)
	381 (1762-1814)
1st Foot, Royal Scots 2nd Battalion	74 (1737-1801)
2nd Foot, Queen's Royal Regiment (West Surrey)	2 (1818) in lieu of 244 (1754-1825)
	390 (1762-1815)
4th Foot, King's Own Royal Regiment (Lancaster)	4 (1818) in lieu of 50
	91 (1857-1876)
	522 (1785-1823)
5th Foot, Royal Northumberland Fusiliers	86 (1738-1815)
6th Foot, Royal Warwickshire	45 (1735-1801)
	643 (1785-1800)
	646 (1785-1818)
7th Foot, Royal Fusiliers (City of London)	231 (1752-1801)
9th Foot, Royal Norfolk	246 (1754-1817)
10th Foot, Lincolnshire	177 (1748-55)
	299 (1758-1803)
	378 (1761-1815)
11th Foot, Devonshire	604 (1782-94)
13th Foot, Somerset Light Infantry	637 (1784-1818)
	661 (1787-1819)
14th Foot, West Yorkshire (Prince of Wales Own)	211 (1750-1815)

15th Foot, East Yorkshire	245 (1754-1801)
16th Foot, Bedfordshire & Hertfordshire	293 (1758-1817)
	300 (1758-1801)
17th Foot, Leicestershire	136 (1743-1801)
	921 (1802-1824)
	258 (1824), in lieu of 921 (1847)
18th Foot, Royal Irish	168 (1747-1801)
	351 (1760-1818)
19th Foot, Green Howards	156 (1747-1779)
20th Foot, Lancashire Fusiliers, 1st Battalion	63 (1737-1869)
20th Foot, Lancashire Fusiliers, 2nd Battalion	263 (1860-1907)
21st Foot, Royal Scots Fusiliers	33 (1734-1801)
	936 (1803-1817)
	exchanged for 33 (1817-1864)
22nd Foot, Cheshire	251 (1754-1817)
23rd Foot, Royal Welsh Fusiliers	738 (1808-1821)
	revived (1882-1892)
25th Foot, King's Own Scottish Borderers	92 (1738-1815)
	250 (1819-1823)
	exchanged for 25 (1823-1839)
26th Foot, 1st Battalion, The Cameronians	309 (1758)
	exchanged for 26 (1810-1823) & (1823-1922)
27th Foot, 1st Battalion, Royal Inniskilling Fusiliers	24 (1734-1801)
	205 (1750-1785)
	528 (1787-1815)
	692 (1808-1818)
28th Foot, 1st Battalion, Gloucestershire	35 (1734-1801)
	510 (1773-1858)
28th Foot, 2nd Battalion, Gloucestershire	260 (1809-15)
29th Foot, 1st Battalion, Worcestershire	322 (1759-)
30th Foot, 1st Battalion, East Lancashire	85 (1738-1793 exchanged for 30, (1805-1823), 535 (1776-)
32nd Foot, 1st Battalion, Duke of Cornwall's Light Infantry	61 (1736-1801), 617 (1783-1815), 524 (1921-37)
33rd Foot, 1st Battalion, Duke of Wellington's	12 (1732-1817)
35th Foot, 1st Battalion, Royal Sussex	205 (1749-90)

36th Foot	542 (1770-80)
	559 (1778-)
38th Foot, 1st Battalion, South Staffordshire	38 (1734-1801)
	441 (1765-1840)
39th Foot, 1st Battalion, Dorsetshire	128 (1742-1886)
	290 (1758-1815)
40th Foot, 1st Battalion, Prince of Wales Volunteers (South Lancs.)	204 (1810-1813)
	284 (1821-1858)
42nd Foot, 1st Battalion, Black Watch (Royal Highlanders)	42 (1809-1840)
	195 (1749-1815)
44th Foot, 1st Battalion, Essex	788 (1793-)
45th Foot, 1st Battalion, Sherwood Foresters	445 (1766-1815)
46th Foot, 2nd Battalion, Duke of Cornwall's Light Infantry	174 (1896-1921)
	227 (1752-1847)
47th Foot, 1st Battalion, The Loyal Regiment (North Lancashire)	147 (1810-1823)
	192 (1748-1823)
48th Foot, 1st Battalion, Northamptonshire	86 (1738-1784)
	218 (1750-1858)
	631 (1784-1818)
	982 (1806-17)
49th Foot, 1st Battalion, Royal Berkshire	354 (1760-1851)
	616 (1783-1817)
50th Foot, 1st Battalion, Queen's Own Royal West Kent	58 (1857-1876)
	113 (1763-1815)
51st Foot, 1st Battalion, King's Own Yorks. Light Infantry	94 (1761-1815)
	690 (1788-96)
52nd Foot, 2nd Battalion, Oxford and Bucks Light Infantry	244 (1832-1845)
	370 (1761-1825)
53rd Foot, 1st Battalion, King's Shropshire Light Infantry	236 (1773-1815)
	950 (1804-24)
56th Foot, 2nd Battalion, Essex	420 (1765-1817)
58th Foot, 2nd Battalion, Northamptonshire	466 (1769-1816)
	692 (1789-1808)
59th Foot, 2nd Battalion, East Lancashire	219 (1810-1819)
	243 (1754-1815)
62nd Foot, 1st Battalion, Wiltshire (Duke of Edinburgh)	407 (1763-86)
63rd Foot, 1st Battalion, Manchester	512 (1774-1814)
64th Foot, 1st Battalion, North Staffordshire (Prince of Wales)	130 (1817-58)
	686 (1788) exchanged for 130 (1817)
65th Foot, 1st Battalion, York and Lancaster	631 (1784-1818)
66th Foot, 2nd Battalion, Royal Berkshire	392 (1763-1817)

	538 (1777-1811)
	580 (1780-1817)
66th Foot, 2nd Battalion, Royal Berkshire	656 (1808) (unconfirmed)
67th Foot, 2nd Battalion, Royal Berkshire	388 (1762-1813)
68th Foot, 1st Battalion, Durham Light Infantry	714 (1790-1815)
69th Foot, 2nd Battalion, The Welsh	174 (1791-1821)
	983 (1807-36)
70th Foot, 2nd Battalion, East Surrey	770 (1871-75)
71st Foot, 1st Battalion, Highland Light Infantry	895 (1801-58)
72nd Foot, 1st Battalion, Seaforth Highlanders	65 (1854-60)
75th Foot, 1st Battalion, Gordon Highlanders	292 (1810-25)
76th Foot, 2nd Battalion, Gordon Highlanders	359 (1760-1763)
77th Foot, Atholl Highlanders	578 (1780-1818)
82nd Foot, 2nd Battalion, Prince of Wales Volunteers	138 (1817-58)
83rd Foot, (1758 – 1763)	339 (1759-64)
83rd Foot, 1st Battalion, Royal Ulster Rifles	435 (1808) exchanged for 83 (1817)
83rd Foot, 16th Service Battalion, Royal Irish Rifles	420 (1915-21)
87th Foot, 7th Service Battalion, Royal Irish Fusiliers	415 (1915-1924)
88th Foot, 1st Battalion, Connaught Rangers	19 (1907-20)
	176 (1821-71)
89th Foot 2nd Battalion, Royal Irish Fusiliers	538 (1811-15)
	863 (1798-1818)
92nd Foot, Donegal Light Infantry	364 (1761-63)
96th/97th Foot, Queen's Germans	984 (1807-1818 exchanged for 176, (1818-19)
103rd Foot, Bombay European Regiment	292 (1834-56)
112th Foot, Lord Donoughmore's	815 (1795-1815)
4th Foot, Garrison Battalion	986 (1810-15)
5th Foot, Garrison Battalion	125 (1808-14)
7th Foot, Garrison Battalion	992 (1808-15)
8th Foot, Garrison Battalion	995 (1808-14)
4th Foot, Veteran Battalion	988 (1808-15)
Commissariat Corps	203 (1809-15)
West Africa Regiment	157 (1908-28)
West India Regiment	390 (1905-27)
Colonel Pool's Regiment	177 (1748-55)
Colonel Folliott's Regiment	168 (1747-01)
Hon Brigadier Guise's Regiment	45 (1801); no GLI record.

Colonel Hamilton's Regiment	23 (1733-1801)
Colonel Lascelle's Regiment	192 (1749-1823)
Militia Regiments	
Antrim	289 (1796-1856)
Armagh	888 (1800-45)
Carlow	903 (1801-16)
Cavan	300 (1801-16)
South Cork	495 (1794-15)
City of Cork	741 (1806-17)
Donegal	865 (1798-1821
Downshire	212 (1795-1813)
South Down	214 (1810-15)
City of Dublin	62 (1810-21)
Fermanagh	864 (1798-1830)
Kerry	66 (1810-29)
Kildare	847 (1797-1825)
Kilkenny	855 (1797-1825)
King's County	948 (1804-16)
Leitrim	854 (1797-1868)
Longford	304 (1807-26)
Louth	10 (1809-49)
Mayo South	79 (1810-30)
	81 (1812-25)
Meath	50 (not issued)
	898 (1801-49)
Monaghan	200 (1801-16)
	552 (1796-1816)
Queen's County	398 (1805-10)
	857 (1797-1832)
Roscommon	242 (1808-17)
Sligo	837 (1796-1835)
South Lincoln	867 (1799-1813)
Tipperary	856 (1797-1825)
Tyrone	225 (1808-14)
	562 (1797-1817)
	846 (1796-1818)
Waterford	961 (1805-16)
Westmeath	50, 791 (1793-1826)
Wexford	935 (1803-24)
Wicklow	848 (1796-1815)

	877 (1800-18)
Royal Independent Dublin Volunteers	620 (1783-...)
Fencible Regiments	
1st Fencible Light Dragoons	384 (1799-1802)
Ulster Provincial Regiment of Foot	612 (1783-...)
Breadalbane	907 (1801-13)
Elgin	860 (1798-1813)
Essex	852 (1796-1813)
Fife	861 (1798-1804)

Military Warrants Issued by the Grand Lodge of the Antients

Cavalry Regiments	
3rd Dragoons, R A Union	197 (1806-)
6th Dragoons	123 (1763-)
6th Dragoons	311 (1797-1837
7th Dragoons	262 (1807-24)
9th Dragoons	284 (1794-1813)
11th Dragoons	339 (1807-10)
17th Dragoons	285 (1794-1828)
Artillery	
1st Battalion Royal Artillery, Scotland	134 (1764-74)
1st Battalion Royal Artillery, Chatham	187 (1774-77)
1st Battalion Royal Artillery, Gibraltar	230 (1785-)
2nd Battalion Royal Artillery, Perth	148 (1767-)
4th Battalion Royal Artillery, New York	213 (1781-)
4th Battalion Royal Artillery, New York	144 (1804-)
4th Battalion Royal Artillery, Gibraltar	209 (1779-)
4th Battalion Royal Artillery, Gibraltar	345 (1809-27)
5th Battalion Royal Artillery, Eastbourne	101 (1812-23)
6th Battalion Royal Artillery, Sri Lanka	329 (1802-30)
9th Battalion Royal Artillery, Gibraltar	187 (1812-22)
10th Battalion Royal Artillery, South Africa	354 (1812-51)
10th Battalion Royal Artillery, Gibraltar	356 (1813-21)
Royal Horse Artillery, Colchester	156 (1809-28)
RHA, Woolwich	86 (1761-)

Capt. Webdell's Company	183 (1773-)
Quebec, St John	241 (1787-)
Port Royal, Jamaica	262 (1790-1805)
Kolkata (Calcutta)	317 (1798-)
Quebec	40 (1804-14)

Infantry Regiments

3rd	170 (1771-92)
5th, St George	353 (1812-62)
7th	153 (1804-)
9th	183 (1803-29)
11th	72 (1758-67)
11th	313 (1798-1813)
13th	153 (1768-76)
14th	58 (1759-1813)
14th, Union	338 (1807-30)
14th, Officers' Lodge	347 (1810-13)
17th	237 (1787-92)
18th	335 (1806-13)
23rd	252 (1788-1822)
33rd	90 (1761-1813)
34th	340 (1807-32)
37th	52 (1756-1813)
40th	42 (no date)
45th	272 (1792-1807)
50th	112 (17763-1830)
51st, Orange	94 (1763-1805)
52nd	309 (1797-1801)
52nd	170 (1801-13)
57th	41 (1755-)
58th	332 (1805-23)
65th	191 (1774-)
67th	175 (1772-)
68th, Durham Light	348 (1810-44)
72nd	75 (1759-64)
76th	248 (1788-1828)
78th	322 (1801-30)
79th, Waterloo	191 (1808-38)
85th	298 (1801-46)
91st, Argyle	321 (1799-1828)
92nd	333 (1805-32)

96th	170 (undated)
Engineers	
Artificers, Jersey	293 (1795)
RM Artificers, Jersey	350 (1810)

Overseas Lodges Warranted by the Grand Lodge of Ireland

Warrant No.	Location	Country	Date
148	Norwich	England	24.06.1745
247	London	England	08.05.1754
252	Paisley	Scotland	10.12.1754
123	Douglas	Isle of Man	12.03.1857
458	Douglas	Isle of Man	03.12.1767
212	Castletown	Isle of Man	08.06.1857
221	Peel	Isle of Man	05.11.1858
265	St. Aubin, Jersey	Channel Islands	02.03.1820
325	Gibraltar	Gibraltar	07.09.1826
328	Gibraltar	Gibraltar	05.03.1885
915	Gibraltar	Gibraltar	--.11.1991
273	Senglea	Malta	01.06.1899
387	Malta	Malta	21.11.1851
347	Algeciras	Spain	07.04.1843
503	Beziers	France	05.08.1773
338	Lisbon	Portugal	27.06.1839
339	Lisbon	Portugal	04.02.1842
341	Lisbon	Portugal	31.03.1843
344	Lisbon	Portugal	15.03.1844
166	Buyukdore, Istanbul	Turkey	31.01.1865
151	Lima	Peru	13.11.1861

157	Lima	Peru	09.07.1863
378	Maranhao	Brazil	07.03.1856
300	Bangkok	Thailand	04.10.1900
62	Colombo	Sri Lanka	04.10.1821
107	Colombo	Sri Lanka	16.02.1861
112	Colombo	Sri Lanka	19.01.1864
115	Colombo	Sri Lanka	02.05.1868
298	Dimbula	Sri Lanka	28.05.1874
263	Calcutta	India	11.10.1909
319	Bombay	India	03.04.1911
357	Kurnaul	India	31.07.1837
382	Calcutta	India	03.05.1905
408	Bombay	India	06.10.1913
419	Bombay	India	05.06.1915
458	Simla	India	06 06.1919
464	Calcutta	India	08.10.1919
465	Calcutta	India	08.10.1919
490	Calcutta	India	16.10.1920
567	Calcutta	India	18.07.1924
648	Bombay	India	10.10.1933
768	New Delhi	India	07.10.1954
771	Bombay	India	03.03.1955
792	Matheran, Bombay	India	04.10.1956
794	Bombay	India	Not known
804	Bombay	India	05.06.1958
807	Bombay	India	05.03.1959
815	Calcutta	India	02.06.1960
830	Kuala Lumpur	Malaysia	03.03.1966
765	Singapore	Singapore	04.03.1954
463	Shanghai	China	08.10.1919
712	Hong Kong	Hong Kong	09.12.1946
883	Hong Kong	Hong Kong	-- --- 1981
123	Hamilton	Bermuda	11.06.1908
209	St. George's	Bermuda	15.08.1881
220	St. George's	Bermuda	05.09.1856

224	St. George's	Bermuda	18.02.1867
580	Hamilton	Bermuda	07.03.1924
894	Warwick	Bermuda	-- --- 1986
235	Port Louis	Mauritius	05.11.1858
236	Port Louis	Mauritius	20.05.1878
266	Port Louis	Mauritius	18.01.1888
222	Barbados	Barbados	06.06.1822
259	Barbados	Barbados	06.06.1822
277	Barbados	Barbados	06.06.1822
282	Barbados	Barbados	05.05.1842
622	Bridgetown	Barbados	02.10.1783
653	Barbados	Barbados	02.12.1802
35	Kingston	Jamaica	07.04.1814
390	Kingston	Jamaica	16.12.1927
456	Kingston	Jamaica	05.10.1767
699	Kingston	Jamaica	03.09.1789
733	Port Royal	Jamaica	07.04.1791
738	St. Jago	Jamaica	02.06.1791
889	Kingston	Jamaica	-- --- 1984
921	Kingston	Jamaica	-- --- 1996
223	Castries	St. Lucia	20.02.1847
224	St. George's	Grenada	30.10.1848
252	St. George's	Grenada	04.11.1819
157	West African Regiment		02.10.1908
157	Accra	Ghana	08.10.1977
110	Jagersfontein	South Africa	25.11.1907
159	Johannesburg	South Africa	08.03.1895
199	Cape Town	South Africa	02.10.1896
214	Selukwe	South Africa	11.10.1909
247	Johannesburg	South Africa	06.06.1898
265	Jeppestown	South Africa	06.03.1899
277	Fordsburgh	South Africa	09.10.1899
288	Maraisburg	South Africa	06.06.1910
323	Bensoni	South Africa	12.03.1912
338	Germiston	South Africa	07.03.1903

344	Randfontein	South Africa	31.03.1913
360	Cape Town	South Africa	03.10.1903
361	Pretoria	South Africa	03.10.1903
364	Fordsburg	South Africa	05.10.1903
365	Durban	South Africa	05.10.1903
368	Cape Town	South Africa	05.10.1903
391	Germiston	South Africa	14.11.1905
339	Pretoria	South Africa	12.06.1906
400	Johannesburg	South Africa	12.06.1906
523	Springs	South Africa	06.12.1921
576	Bellevue	South Africa	07.03.1924
576	Johannesburg	South Africa	18.11.1964
608	Sea Point, Cape Town	South Africa	09.03.1927
610	Milnerton, Cape Town	South Africa	09.03.1927
653	Cape Town	South Africa	11.06.1935
671	Wynberg, Cape Town	South Africa	11.12.1939
710	Primrose, Germiston	South Africa	09.12.1946
729	Van Der Bujl Park	South Africa	07.10.1948
743	Pretoria	South Africa	06.06.1950
767	Johannesburg	South Africa	04.03.1954
773	Duiwelskloof	South Africa	02.06.1955
832	Johannesburg	South Africa	01.03.1967
852	Pietersburg	South Africa	07.06.1973
853	Kempton Park	South Africa	07.06.1973
855	Rewlatch, Johannesburg	South Africa	29.09.1973
858	Boksburg South	South Africa	-- --- 1975
862	White River	South Africa	-- --- 1975
873	Port Elizabeth	South Africa	14.10.1978
878	Brakpan	South Africa	-- --- 1979
879	Witbank	South Africa	-- --- 1979
200	Perth Western Australia	Australia	05.12.1896
233	Perth	Australia	09.10.1897
260	Sydney New South Wales	Australia	06.01.1820
266	Sydney	Australia	12.08.1824
267	Sydney	Australia	29.01.1845
275	Windsor	Australia	18.02.1843
277	Sydney	Australia	28.07.1884
278	Parramatta	Australia	18.02.1863
290	St. Leonards, Sydney	Australia	18.07.1867
292	Pietermaritzburg	Australia	17.10.1910

294	Kiama	Australia	15.05.1873
296	Hill End	Australia	21.05.1873
303	Richmond	Australia	10.07.1884
279	Brisbane Queensland	Australia	19.02.1864
283	Brisbane	Australia	19.06.1865
285	Fortitude Valley	Australia	18.05.1865
286	South Brisbane	Australia	17.10.1865
287	Ipswich	Australia	17.05.1866
288	Ipswich	Australia	19.07.1866
289	Townsville	Australia	18.12.1866
291	Toowoomba	Australia	26.12.1872
292	Maryborough	Australia	14.04.1870
293	Stanthorpe	Australia	10.02.1873
312	Beenleigh	Australia	03.10.1878
318	MacKay	Australia	02.12.1880
319	Fortitude Valley	Australia	11.12.1884
323	Bundaberg	Australia	--.04.1886
328	Normantown	Australia	03.06.1886
329	Gympie	Australia	20.10.1885
330	Brisbane	Australia	18.01.1888
331	South Brisbane	Australia	04.10.1888
337	Red Hill	Australia	06.12.1889
338	Charters Towers	Australia	06.12.1889
339	Woolloongabba	Australia	02.10.1890
340	Charters Towers	Australia	03.10.1891
341	Redcliff	Australia	07.06.1895
342	Wynnum	Australia	07.06.1893
343	Brisbane	Australia	02.10.1896
344	Rockhampton	Australia	07.12.1896
345	Queenton	Australia	01.06.1899
346	Toowoomba	Australia	07.03.1901
347	Ballenden	Australia	06.03.1902
349	Townsville	Australia	06.03.1902
353	Mount Morgan	Australia	05.06.1903
363	Adelaide South Australia	Australia	07.11.1855
406	Salisbury	Australia	03.12.1858
408	Norwood & Kensington	Australia	10.09.1860
410	Kapunda	Australia	14.12.1860
412	Goolwa	Australia	09.07.1868
415	Penola	Australia	04.09.1869

416	Auburn		Australia	08.03.1870
455	Adelaide		Australia	12.05.1871
457	Narracoorte		Australia	06.01.1877
461	Riverton		Australia	16.05.1878
349	Melbourne	Victoria	Australia	30.04.1847
368	Melbourne		Australia	11.08.1857
380	Melbourne		Australia	09.08.1858
370	E. Collingwood		Australia	11.01.1858
386	Moonee Ponds		Australia	03.03.1858
391	Forest Creek		Australia	16.03.1858
413	Buninyong		Australia	07.02.1859
422	Melbourne		Australia	21.08.1860
423	Ararat		Australia	07.05.1860
424	Prahan		Australia	08.05.1860
425	Clunes		Australia	09.05.1860
426	Linton		Australia	18.03.1862
427	Ballarat		Australia	19.05.1862
428	Prahan		Australia	17.12.1862
429	Hotham		Australia	19.02.1863
434	Smythesdale		Australia	19.02.1863
436	Talbot		Australia	14.07.1863
439	Ballarat		Australia	19.10.1863
440	Beechworth		Australia	18.05.1864
443	Taradale		Australia	19.04.1865
444	Matlock		Australia	18.12.1865
452	Sebastopol		Australia	08.07.1870
458	Fitzroy		Australia	21.09.1876
459	Melbourne		Australia	21.09.1876
467	Melbourne		Australia	03.10.1879
474	Prahan		Australia	03.02.1887
476	Bacchus		Australia	07.03.1889
477	Melbourne		Australia	19.03.1889
313	Hobart	Tasmania	Australia	03.09.1829
326	Hobart		Australia	04.03.1833
345	Hobart		Australia	--.11.1834
346	Launceston		Australia	14.06.1843
347	Oatlands		Australia	21.10.1872
353	Beaconsfield		Australia	21.07.1884
354	Deloraine		Australia	21.07.1884
358	Launceston		Australia	21.07.1884

359	Ringarooma		Australia	21.07.1884
360	Formby		Australia	01.07.1886
361	Longford		Australia	03.02.1887
362	Hobart		Australia	02.03.1888
348	Auckland		New Zealand	05.09.1842
419	Napier		New Zealand	08.10.1858
420	Onehunga		New Zealand	16.12.1863
421	Auckland		New Zealand	25.05.1864
446	New Plymouth		New Zealand	19.05.1865
448	Dunedin		New Zealand	19.06.1866
449	Cambridge		New Zealand	18.05.1866
450	Hamilton		New Zealand	24.05.1861
454	Thames Gold Fields		New Zealand	19.10.1870
456	Coromandel		New Zealand	22.10.1872
462	Tauranga		New Zealand	31.12.1877
463	Christchurch		New Zealand	16.05.1878
464	Waipukurau		New Zealand	20.05.1878
465	Gisborne		New Zealand	10.12.1878
468	Dunedin		New Zealand	01.12.1881
469	Wellington		New Zealand	05.10.1882
471	Invercargill		New Zealand	23.10.1883
472	Gisborne		New Zealand	30.12.1886
475	Petone		New Zealand	04.04.1888
478	Blenheim		New Zealand	29.06.1889
480	Waiuku		New Zealand	06.10.1893
227	Montreal	Quebec	Canada	02.07.1847
237	Quebec		Canada	09.06.1854
159	Hawksbury	Ontario	Canada	15.03.1844
211	Port Stanley		Canada	31.10.1850
222	Toronto		Canada	03.12.1847
226	Ingersoll		Canada	30.08.1851
231	Hamilton		Canada	02.07.1852
232	St. Thomas		Canada	30.03.1853
236	Nobleville		Canada	08.05.1854
238	Dunville		Canada	17.07.1854
283	Kingston		Canada	01.02.1821
286	York		Canada	10.12.1850
323	Brantford		Canada	06.06.1853
358	Binbrook		Canada	08.01.1855

359	Stratford	Canada	10.03.1855
301	St John's New Brunswick	Canada	10.04.1837
318	St. Andrew's	Canada	10.03.1830
324	Portland	Canada	14.05.1842
327	St. Stephen's	Canada	17.03.1846
347	Carleton	Canada	07.10.1859
330	Amherst Nova Scotia	Canada	10.01.1845
331	Halifax	Canada	15.04.1853
399	New York	U.S.A.	07.07.1763

Following the establishment of grand lodges internationally, the majority of Irish-warranted lodges working overseas returned their warrants to the Grand Lodge of Ireland and applied to join their national grand lodge.

Many of those warrants were subsequently cancelled, however, others were reissued by the Grand Lodge of Ireland to both domestic and overseas lodges.

One example is the warrant for lodge No.110. First issued in 1739 to an Irish lodge, it was cancelled, reissued, returned, and reissued again, before being granted to Union Lodge, Jagersfontein, South Africa, in 1907. The warrant was surrendered by Union Lodge in 1920 and returned to Ireland where it was allocated to the Provincial Grand Master's Peace Lodge meeting at Freemasons' Hall, Newtownards Road, Belfast.

Certain lodges, including those in Bermuda, the Caribbean, India, South Africa, Sri Lanka and Zambia, as well as in South East Asia, continue to operate under provincial grand lodges constituted by the Grand Lodge of Ireland, while others remain under the direct authority of Dublin itself.[102]

---

[102] Irish & Antients Military Lodges and Overseas Lodges of the Grand Lodge of Ireland, principal sources: Antients Grand Lodge, *Register of Warranted Lodges*; Grand Lodge of Ireland, *Register of Warranted Lodges*; Robert Freke Gould, *Military Lodges, The Apron and the Sword* (London: Gale and Polden Ltd, 1899); Lepper & Crossle, *History of the Grand Lodge of Ireland*; and John Lane, *Masonic Records 1717-1894*, https://www.dhi.ac.uk/lane/.

Ric Berman

The Prestonian Lecture – A History

The Prestonian Lecture is the only official lecture held under the authority of the United Grand Lodge of England. The lecturer is appointed on the nomination of the Board of General Purposes by the Trustees of the Prestonian Fund and the lecture is given officially on at least four occasions, and at least twice in London. The lecture is also given unofficially during and after the Prestonian year both in Great Britain and overseas. Lodges who wish to host the lecture officially do so by contacting the grand secretary through Metropolitan, Provincial or District Grand Secretaries.

The Lectureship is a memorial to William Preston (1742-1818), an author, printer and the foremost masonic educator of his age, who left a legacy to Grand Lodge for this purpose.

Lectures were given in Preston's name from 1820 until 1862, when the programme went into abeyance. The Prestonian Lectureship was revived in 1924 with the modification that the lecturer would give a talk on a subject of his own choosing. The Prestonian Lecture has been given annually since that date, with the exception of the period 1940-46.

William Preston was born in Edinburgh on 28 July 1742 and educated at the Royal High School and the University of Edinburgh. He took employment as secretary to the classicist and grammarian Thomas

Ruddiman (1654-1757), who, suffering from poor health, arranged for Preston to be apprenticed to his brother, Walter, a printer and publisher.

Armed with a letter of introduction from Walter Ruddiman, Preston moved to London in 1760 where he obtained work with William Strahan (1715-1785), later the King's Printer.

Preston was employed initially as a 'principal corrector' and over time rose steadily through the ranks, being promoted to superintendent and thereafter editor. In 1804, Strahan's son, Andrew, who had inherited the business from his father, made Preston a partner in the firm. Strahan was one of the largest print houses in London and reputedly the most profitable, printing and publishing a broad range of popular and notable authors and as it expanded Preston benefited accordingly.

Preston's interest in freemasonry appears to date from the early 1760s when a group of Edinburgh men resident in London formed a masonic lodge, No.111, under the auspices of the Antients Grand Lodge. The lodge was warranted in 1763 and met at the White Hart tavern in the Strand. A year later, the lodge took a new constitution under the auspices of the Moderns and a new name, Caledonian Lodge.

The Moderns' warrant, No.325, was granted on 15 November 1764. The lodge met at the Half Moon Tavern on Cheapside in the City of London. The lodge still exists and is now No.134, meeting at Mark Masons' Hall, 86 St James's Street, London.

Preston was reportedly the second man to be initiated into the lodge and was reputedly instrumental in the transfer of jurisdiction from 'Antients' to 'Moderns'. On becoming master of the lodge he undertook 'To inform myself fully of the general rules of the Society, that I might be able to fulfil my own duty and officially enforce obedience in others.'

Preston subsequently became master of several other London lodges and simultaneously began to develop a series of lectures to explain the different masonic degrees. The success of his orations was such that he was able to publish his lectures in 1772 as *Illustrations of Freemasonry*. The work ran to some seventeen editions and was complemented by a series of catechetical lectures explaining the three Craft degrees.

In 1774, Preston visited the Lodge of Antiquity, previously the Goose & Gridiron and one of the four lodges that had founded the Grand Lodge of England. He was invited to become a joining member in June 1774 and, possibly as a means of arresting a decline in membership numbers, was within two weeks invited to become master.

The lodge flourished during Preston's three and a half years as Worshipful Master and his status was acknowledged by his appointment as deputy grand secretary and 'Printer to the Society'.

The reputation of the Lodge of Antiquity was enhanced further when the Duke of Sussex, the first grand master of the United Grand Lodge of England, became a member and master of the lodge.

In December 1777, in part because of personal disputes within the lodge, Preston and other members of the Lodge of Antiquity were reported to Grand Lodge for apparently disregarding standing orders by appearing in public in their masonic regalia. They were accused of taking part in a masonic procession albeit that they were simply returning to the Lodge from a nearby church service. A formal complaint against them was investigated and Preston was expelled after claiming that the Lodge of Antiquity as a 'time immemorial' lodge pre-dated the Grand Lodge and was not subject to its rules.

Preston subsequently led a breakaway group from the Lodge of Antiquity and an authority was sought and subsequently obtained from a rival grand lodge – the Grand Lodge of York – to establish 'the Grand Lodge of England South of the River Trent', of which Preston later became deputy grand master. The dispute was resolved a decade later in May 1789 with Preston offering an apology. Honour satisfied, Preston was welcomed back to the Grand Lodge of England and in 1790 the Lodge of Antiquity was re-united.

William Preston died on 1 April 1818 at his home at Dean Street, London, and was buried on 10 April in St Paul's Churchyard by St Paul's Cathedral. Under the terms of his Will he bequeathed an endowment of £300 to the United Grand Lodge of England to provide for the annual delivery of a lecture, the lecturer to be appointed by the trustees and charged with delivering an address on a masonic subject that will 'instruct and entertain a general Lodge audience'.

Prestonian Lecturers, 1924-2024

1924 — C.W. Firebrace
The First Degree

1925 — L. Vibert
The Development of the Trigradal System

1926 — L. Vibert
The Evolution of the Second Degree

1927 — G.P.G. Hills
Bro William Preston: the Man, his Methods & Work

1928 — J. Stokes
Masonic Teachers of the Eighteenth Century

1929 — R.H. Baxter
The Antiquity of Our Masonic Legends

1930 — H.D. de Lafontaine
The Seven Liberal Arts and Sciences

1931 — W. Covey Crump
Medieval Master Masons and their Secrets

1932 — J.H. Lepper
The Evolution of Masonic Ritual in England in the Eighteenth Century

1933 — H. Poole
The Old Charges in Eighteenth Century Masonry

1934 — F.C.C.M. Fighiera
The Art, Craft, Science, or 'Mystery' of Masonry

1935 — W.J. Bunney
Freemasonry and Contemplative Art

1936 — L. Edwards
Freemasonry, Ritual and Ceremonial

1937 — J. Johnson
Inwardness of Masonic Symbolism in the Three Degrees

1938 — D. Knoop
The Mason Word

1939 — G.E.W. Bridge
Veiled in Allegory and Illustrated by Symbols

1940-1946 — Suspended

1947 — G.Y. Johnson
The Grand Lodge South of the River Trent

1948	F.L. Pick
The Deluge	
1949	C.C. Adams
Our Oldest Lodge	
1950	W.I. Grantham
Lodges of Instruction, their Origin and Development	
1951	H.W. Chetwin
Variations in Masonic Ceremonial	
1952	B.E. Jones
Free in Freemason: The Idea of Freedom through Six Centuries	
1953	G.S. Shepherd-Jones
What is Freemasonry?	
1954	B.W. Oliver
The Freemason's Education	
1955	J.R. Rylands
The Fellowship of Knowledge	
1956	G.S. Draffen
The Making of a Mason	
1957	H. Carr
The Transition from Operative to Speculative Masonry	
1958	N. Rogers
The Years of Development	
1959	J.S. Purvis
Medieval Organisation of Freemasons' Lodges	
1960	S. Pope
Growth of Freemasonry in England & Wales since 1717	
1961	G. Brett
King Solomon in the Middle Ages	
1962	P.R. James
The Grand Mastership of HRH the Duke of Sussex	
1963	H.G.M. Clarke
Folklore into Masonry	
1964	A.J. Arkell
The Genesis of Freemasonry	
1965	E. Newton
Brethren who Made Masonic History	
1966	W.R.S. Bathurst
The Evolution of the English Provincial Grand Lodge	
1967	A.R. Hewitt
The Grand Lodge of England: the First Hundred Years	

1968	H.K. Atkins
The Five Noble Orders of Architecture	
1969	J.R. Clarke
External Influences on the Evolution of English Masonry	
1970	E. Ward
In the Beginning was the Word	
1971	R. Tydeman
Masters and Master Masons	
1972	T.O. Haunch
'It is not in the power of any man': a Study in Change	
1973	C.F.W. Dyer
In Search of Ritual Uniformity	
1974	N. Barker Cryer
Drama and Craft	
1975	T. Beck
Anthony Sayer, Gentleman: the Truth at Last	
1976	A.C.F. Jackson
Preston's England	
1977	R.A. Wells
The Tyler or Outer Guard	
1978	C. Mackechnie-Jarvis
Grand Stewards 1728-1978	
1979	G.E. Walker
250 Years of Masonry in India	
1980	F.J. Cooper
Robert Freke Gould	
1981	C.N. Batham
Grand Lodge of England According to the Old Institutions	
1982	J. Stubbs
The Government of the Craft	
1983	R.H.S. Rottenbury
The Pre-Eminence of the Great Architect in Freemasonry	
1984	H. Mendoza
Getting and Giving Masonic Knowledge	
1985	S. Bruce
'not only Ancient but useful and necessary': Deacons	
1986	W. McLeod
The Old Charges	
1987	C. Gotch
The Role of the Innkeeper in Masonry	

Year	Author	Title
1988	A.I. Pearmain	Music and Masonry
1989	Sir L. Brett	The Book of Constitutions of UGLE
1990	F. Smyth	The Master-Mason-at-Arms
1991	K.T. Flynn	Freemasons at War
1992	M. Morgan	Masonry: Pure and Applied
1993	J.M. Hamill	'And the Greatest of These is Charity'
1994	M.L. Brodsky	English Freemasonry in Europe, 1717-1919
1995	J. Webb	Freemasonry and Sport
1996	J.F. Goodchild	The Freemasons and the Friendly Societies
1997	R.A. Gilbert	The Image of Freemasonry in Popular Fiction
1998	B.F. Page	Elias Ashmole: the First Recorded English Freemason
1999	J.F. Ashby	Freemasonry and Entertainment
2000	R.A. Crane	'for therein you will be taught…'
2001	S. Fernie	The First Degree in Freemasonry
2002	C. Wallis-Newport	The Anglo-Irish Masonic Connections
2003	A.N. Newman	The Contribution of the Provinces to the Development of English Freemasonry
2004	A.T. Stewart	English Freemasonry: Origins, Themes & Developments
2005	G.W.S. Davie	Women and Freemasonry
2006	G.S. Angell	The Victoria Cross – Freemasons' Band of Brothers

2007	R.B.F. Khambatta
Grand Secretaries of the UGLE (1813-1980)	
2008	R. Sillett
The Language of Ritual	
2009	J. Wade
Go and Do Thou Likewise (Masonic Processions)	
2010	W. Warlow
Music in Masonry and Beyond	
2011	J.W.P. Campbell
Was Sir Christopher Wren a Freemason?	
2012	A.D.G. Harvey
Scouting and Freemasonry: Two Parallel Organisations?	
2013	P.R. Calderwood
'As we were seen – the Press and Freemasonry'	
2014	M.A. Kearsley
1814 Consolidation and Change: the first year of the United Grand Lodge of England	
2015	R. Burt
Wherever Dispersed: The Traveling Mason	
2016	R.A. Berman
Foundations: new light on the formation and early years of the Grand Lodge of England	
2017	J.W. Daniel
The Grand Design	
2018	C.P. Noon
A Good Workman Praises His Tools: Masonic Metaphors in the Ancient World	
2019	M. Karn
English Freemasonry during the Great War	
2020	G.R. Boyd-Stones
A 'System of Morality': Aristotle and the Making of Ritual	
2021	G.R. Boyd-Stones
A 'System of Morality': Aristotle and the Making of Ritual	
2022	J.W. Hawkins
Freemasonry and the Royal Family	

2023   A. Elias
The 1723 Constitutions. The Indispensable Trowel:
Cementing America's Foundations'
2024   R.A. Berman
The Second Grand Lodge. The Grand Lodge of Ireland,
the London Irish & Antients Freemasonry

A Prayer to be Repeated at the Making of a New Brother [103]

O God the author and giver of every good and perfect gift and the Grand Architect of the Universe, we thy servants truly sensible of our own unworthiness approach thy Divine Majesty humbly beseeching thee to bless and protect us and all those who with the Secrets of Masonry Endeavour to Unfold and practise the Mysteries of Godliness and Christianity, Grant us Thy Presence in this and all our Undertakings.

Confirm our choice of this thy servant and that he may in all things live as becomes A Mason. Give him the spirit of Wisdom to avoid the Evil and to Choose the good the spirit of Meekness and forbearance and Brotherly love and charity.

Strengthen him against all Temptation that he may Ever be able to Subdue his passions and Adorn us all with the spirit of Zeal for thy Glory, and fervency in thy Worship, that we may not use our Freedom in Christ as A Cloak of Maliciousness but in all our Thoughts Words & Actions so Square our lives within the Compass of thy Commandments, as becomes thy Servants of Christ thy Son, our Lord.

Amen

---

[103] A prayer in long hand on the final page of the Membership Register of Antients' Lodge No.20.

John Murray, 4th Duke of Atholl
GM, Antients Grand Lodge, 1775-81 & 1791-1812
GM, Grand Lodge of Scotland, 1778-1780

The Second Grand Lodge: the 2024 Prestonian Lecture

THE OLD STABLES PRESS

The Old Stables Press
● Oxfordshire ●

www.ingramcontent.com/pod-product-compliance
Lightning Source LLC
Chambersburg PA
CBHW061440040426
42450CB00007B/1144